NEW·IDEAS·FOR
Lap Quilting

GEORGIA BONESTEEL

Oxmoor
House®

Serendipity
by Martha Graves (and she doesn't even quilt!)

Sometimes (heaven help us!) we make a mistake!
    Just the thought of it makes us quiver and quake.

We stitch on a wrong patch or one upside down,
    Or sew on a square when we meant to put round;

Or suddenly the thing goes completely askew
    When we stitch on a patch of impossible hue!

But while we are screaming and having our fit
    We stare at our quilt and we know, "This is it!"

A new pattern's emerged; it's all in new light.
    An amazing thing happened . . . the wrong's become right!

What we thought was so awful, a shame and a pity,
    Becomes something wonderful . . . it's called "serendipity."

I dedicate this book to the creative hands and
minds in public television. A sincere thank you
to Mr. Bill Hannah and The Center for Public
Television, University of North Carolina.

© 1987 by Oxmoor House, Inc.
Book Division of Southern Progress Corporation
P.O. Box 2463, Birmingham, Alabama 35201

Library of Congress Catalog Number: 87-60991
ISBN: 0-8487-0704-4
Manufactured in the United States of America
First Printing 1987

Executive Editor: Candace N. Conard
Production Manager: Jerry Higdon
Associate Production Manager: Rick Litton
Art Director: Bob Nance

New Ideas for Lap Quilting

Editor: Linda Baltzell Wright
Editorial Assistant: Lenda Wyatt
Copy Chief: Mary Jean Haddin
Designer: Diana Smith Morrison
Photographers: Jim Bathie, Colleen Duffley, Gary Clark,
    Howard L. Puckett, Beth Maynor, Mary-Gray Hunter
Artists: Samuel L. Baldwin, Jonathan C. Abercrombie,
    David Morrison

Contents

Introduction

Triangle I

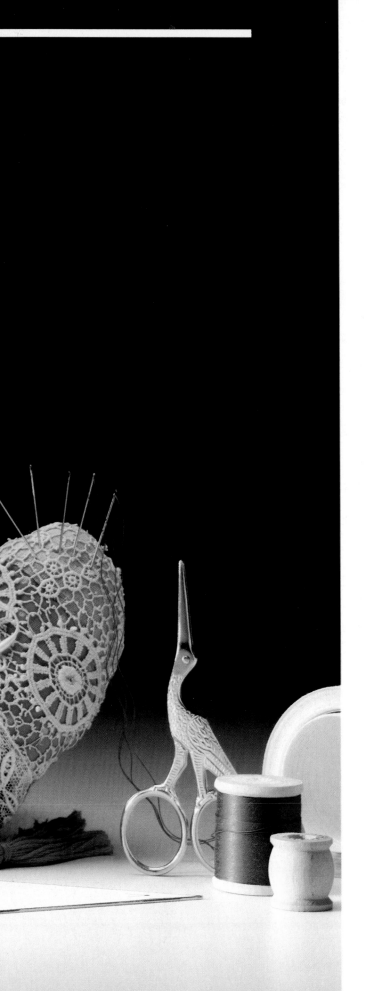

Recently a quilter confessed to me, "Quilters just can't get enough of a good thing." My sentiments exactly! This quilter's heartfelt admission made me realize what a privilege and pleasure it has been for me to be involved with quiltmaking. As a teacher, I'm aware that quilting guidelines and standards have long been established, but I also know that new ideas in quilting abound. There isn't just one way to set a block; there are alternatives waiting to be explored. *New Ideas for Lap Quilting* is the result of my own exploration and is full of options for you to investigate. So sharpen the scissors, preshrink and press that fabric, and get those fingers nimble and ready for all the new ideas.

Quilters discovered cotton years ago and have been experimenting with it ever since. To commemorate cotton's transformation from field to fabric, I designed a cotton boll quilt, complete with boll weevils. As I created the design, a brand-new type of appliqué surfaced—single-surface appliqué. This technique eliminates the extra layers of fabric that make hand quilting difficult.

In the midst of a creative brainstorm, sometimes it's necessary to break the rules. This can lead to unexpected fortune, as it did for my sister, Jill. Many quilters would say it's madness to use madras in a quilt, but Jill and I found that choosing the right pattern was the key to success. In fact, after you review a few special tricks in this book, even your checks and wools will find successful homes in quilts.

My biggest discovery has been freezer paper patchwork. No, you don't place your fabric in the freezer or wrap it in paper! This technique will inspire you to create more original designs and will even lead to speedy, precise sewing at the machine.

With *New Ideas for Lap Quilting* as your springboard to new quilting adventures, your world of patch*work* will become a world of patch*fun*.

Cotton Kivvers

Pull up the cotton kivvers; it's going to be a three-dog night!" our ancestors used to say. Those cotton "kivvers" kept them warm on many a long, cold night. Today, although all-cotton batting has been replaced in part by polyester substitutes, we still prefer cotton fabric for our quilt tops and backing.

Every time I see a cotton field in bloom I stare in awe. It seems miraculous that the cotton picked in the field becomes our precious colorful calico. Cotton has been grown, spun, and woven into cloth in our country since the 17th century. Of course, the spinning and weaving that took hours to do by hand is now done quickly by machine. Today we have looms that make more than 100 yards of cloth an hour.

Textile manufacturing is an extremely complex process. The raw fiber from the field is fluffed and cleaned and formed into ropelike strands. Then a carding machine creates strands called slivers. These yarns are wound onto bobbins or huge rolls, in preparation for weaving on a loom. The final product is fabric called greige goods, and it is stored at a finishing plant to await the dyeing and printing processes.

What is the character of cotton that makes it so special? What makes us fondle the bolts and caress those fat quarters (quilt talk for an 18″ x 22″ square of cloth instead of a piece cut 9″ from selvage to selvage)? Cotton is so soft! Even the bales from the field, after they have been ginned, feel soft to the touch. Each tiny cotton fiber is hollow inside and remains porous no matter how it is woven or knitted. Air and water easily pass through it, making it a comfortable fabric. It has "give"—a forgiving quality when you are piecing. Cotton is superstrong! Cotton thread is as strong as a thin steel wire, and it's even stronger when wet. Cotton is very adaptable since it can be made shrinkproof, wrinkle resistant, and fireproof.

Cotton is a natural fiber that takes longer than any other agricultural product to grow and ripen. It is a patient plant destined for a patient craft—quiltmaking. Of course the greatest compliment we can pay to these bolts of fabric is to buy them, coddle them, cut them up, and resew them into a bounty of beautiful quilts.

PATTERN ENLARGEMENT

What better tribute to cotton than a quilt of cotton pods complete with boll weevil accents and a puffy swag border! There are only four appliqué blocks in this quilt, but the cotton design is so big it bursts over the border. In fact, the templates were too large for these pages and had to be reduced.

How to enlarge a pattern is a handy bit of information for a quilter to know. There may be a bank logo, a picture of a favorite pet, a camp emblem, or another unique design that needs to be enlarged sometime. Most of us are not artists, and we need help to scale up a design. There are at least six different methods we can use to tackle this task.

The first five methods for enlarging rely on mechanical means.

1. The opaque projector is an apparatus that allows you to use the actual picture to be altered. It projects that image so that you can trace it.

2. The overhead projector relies on a transparency of the image to be enlarged. To make a transparency, use a special pen and draw the outline of the desired object on an acetate sheet (available at office supply stores). Place it on a light platform, and the image will be projected.

3. There are small inexpensive enlargers that work well in the home. To use one of these machines, your design must be small.

4. Using a slide projector and screen is another possibility. You may already have a 35 mm slide in your collection that you would like to use. If not, you can take a picture of some object you wish to reproduce and have a slide made of it.

5. The pantograph is also an intriguing tool for changing design sizes. It is one of the oldest enlarging tools and is based on a set of overlapping hinged beams. These beams must be tightly anchored to a table. A pointer pin is

Cotton pods burst forth in the field and fabric.

attached at one end of the tool and a pencil or pen attached to the other end. You simply trace the original artwork with the pointer pin, and the pencil attached to the other end makes an enlarged copy.

Most schools and libraries have these five tools and are willing to let you use them. The projectors and small enlargers work best set up on a table with wheels in a darkened room. Then the size of the image can be varied by moving the machine forward or backward.

6. Using a grid or graph is another way to change a design size, for those of us who are not mechanically inclined. When a grid overlays a design, the design can be copied square by square onto a larger grid, thus enlarging the design. By coding the squares across and down one side, it's easy to keep track of the changes. Grid paper for enlarging is available at most craft and fabric stores, or you can use graph paper and outline the desired size of grid.

After enlarging a design, there are occasions in quilting when we need a means to see through fabric or paper to trace or transfer lines. A light source created by a sunny window, a glass tabletop with a light underneath, or a homemade light box can help us do this with ease. To make a light box, position a light source (either a light bulb or a fluorescent lamp) inside of a box with a piece of plexiglass resting on top. Lay your pattern on the plexiglass with the tracing paper on top.

SINGLE-SURFACE APPLIQUÉ

One problem that occurs in appliqué is that as layers are added, bulk is produced, making hand quilting difficult. For the oversized pattern of *The Cotton Boll*, I developed a special appliqué technique that I call single-surface appliqué. In this cutaway method, only slight overlapping occurs where colors meet. To try single-surface appliqué, just follow this step-by-step procedure.

SINGLE-SURFACE APPLIQUÉ

1. Preparing. Enlarge the design if the original is not the desired size.

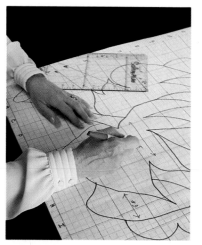

2. Coding. Number each piece in the order to be applied, larger pieces first, then smaller pieces. (The Cotton Boll design has been numbered for you.) Indicate fabric color and grain line, which is parallel to the outside border. This becomes your master paper foundation, a reference for template placement.

3. Making Templates. Place your master paper foundation on your light box, wrong side up. Place a piece of freezer paper, dull side up, over the foundation. Using an indelible pen, trace each shape in the design individually. Also transfer any codes, such as the grain line, color, and numerical sequence. Cut out.

4. Cutting the Pieces. Using a dry iron on a warm setting, press the freezer paper template with the shiny side against the wrong side of the desired fabric. Just cut the rough outline of the template without the indentations. Cut fabric at least ½″ beyond the outside edges of the template. (Approximating is all right.)

5. Positioning Templates. Put foundation fabric on top of master paper foundation (right sides up) and place on light box. Separate freezer paper template from fabric. Use paper foundation as a guide; pin fabric piece on foundation fabric. Trace shape onto fabric piece. Use broken lines in overlap areas.

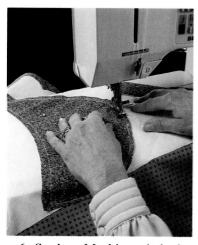

6. Sewing. Machine-stitch the appliqué piece to the foundation along the outline. Use a straight, standard stitch. (Complete steps 6 through 12 for any one template before positioning the next template.)

7. Trimming. Trim the material extending beyond the straight stitching. With pins, mark the areas where the pieces will overlap.

8. Pinning Paper. Pin a piece of typing paper underneath foundation fabric under appliqué piece. This will help keep your satin stitches smooth. Test a satin stitch on a sample fabric to determine desired width of zigzag stitch. Use thread that blends with appliqué figures on both top and bobbin.

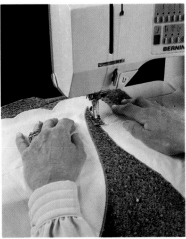

9. Appliquéing. Satin-stitch on the edge of the figure, covering the straight stitching. Gradually narrow your satin stitch as you come to a point. With your needle down, turn your fabric and increase your stitch width as you move away from the point. It isn't necessary to satin-stitch where pieces overlap.

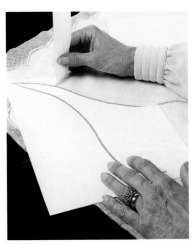

10. Tearing Away Paper. Carefully tear away the typing paper. Remove any small fragments of the paper caught in the stitching.

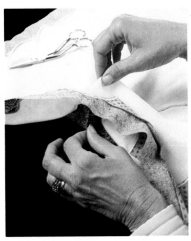

11. Separating the Fabrics. Pull the foundation fabric away from the fabric piece you just appliquéd.

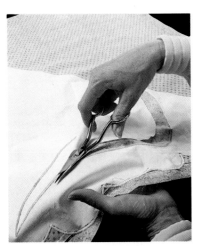

12. Cutting Away Fabric. With appliqué scissors, carefully cut away the foundation fabric underneath the appliqué, trimming up to the satin stitching. Using special appliqué scissors with a lip enables you to achieve a close trim. The scissors can be held with your palm down or with your palm up.

The Cotton Boll

The Cotton Boll quilt combines the two basic techniques of quilting—piecework and appliqué. The borders, the boll weevils, and part of the swag outside border are pieced, using templates and a ¼″ seam allowance. The appliqué portion of *The Cotton Boll* quilt uses my new single-surface appliqué method.

To make one Cotton Boll block, transfer the block design in Figure A to a 2″ grid. This becomes your master paper foundation. Code the paper foundation. Trace and cut out your templates.

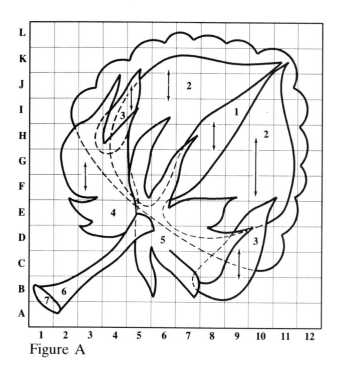

Figure A

Next, cut a 22″ square for the foundation fabric. Then cut four 1¾″ by 24½″ strips for borders. Sew these strips to the square, mitering at the corners. This creates a 24½″ square foundation.

Appliqué the cotton boll to the foundation, following the steps for single-surface appliqué. Begin with shape #1, which is the cotton. After

all shapes are appliquéd, complete three more Cotton Boll blocks. Attach the four blocks together with 5½″ pieced sashing.

Each corner is set off with a boll weevil. With a small hole punch, punch out the ¼″ turns in the boll weevil templates and mark them on the fabric. To piece the boll weevil, sew the triangles to the body. Attach his head to his body, sewing up to the ¼″ turns. With the presser foot up and the needle down, the fabric will swing around, making it easy to sew the next seam. The boll weevil's narrow snout (¼″-wide) extends into the border, where it is appliquéd in place.

Echoing the cotton motif, the swag border completes the quilt. Carefully machine-stitch the two inside curved seams, using a ¼″ seam allowance.

A helpful hint: pinch each cloth curve in the middle and sew from the center outward, aligning raw edges. Attach the white scallop with a machine satin stitch, since the angle is very difficult to piece by machine. Then cut away the back fabric to create a single layer. The corner blocks are divided into triangles for ease in piecing.

The Cotton Boll
Finished Size: 83″ x 83″
Perimeter: 332″
Blocks: Four 24″ appliquéd Cotton Boll blocks
Borders: Four Boll Weevil blocks
   5″ sashing
   10″ x 7″ swag border
   10″ swag corner
Fabric Requirements: Divide amount
   needed by the number of fabrics
   and colors used.
   Foundation and swag border: 3¼ yards
   Backing and binding: 6 yards
   Sashing: 1½ yards green, 1½ yards blue
   Blocks: 1 yard each of gray and green, 3 yards
     white

That's Ducky

In this appliqué quilt, Sunbonnet Sue is making a comeback, but this time she's all wet! So we call this block "Slicker Sue." The image recalls the feel and the smell of the rain slicker and little feet being lost in high rubber galoshes.

Hooray for Betsy Freeman's ingenuity! She has created a charming quilt that takes advantage of lap quilting by staggering bright backings in a diagonal melody of colors. So much color in fact, that she named the back of the quilt *Somewhere Over the Rainbow*. It was even hung backward at a local quilt show. This indicates a new dilemma—how to hang reversible quilts!

If you plan to quilt this design by hand, use the single-surface appliqué method. That way you won't be struggling with the bulk created by so many layers of fabric. Apply the figures to the foundation in the sequence given on the grid design. The broken lines represent black embroidery stitches to accent the block. The quilting lines represent the rain coming down on the imprints of the rubber boots.

The stems of the flowers in the border are strips of 1"-wide bias fabric folded in half. The fabric is inserted in the center seam of the block as it is pieced so that a ¼" strip is exposed. Some of the flower blocks are balanced with plain rectangles.

That's Ducky

Finished Size: 72" x 96"

Perimeter: 336"

Blocks: Twenty-five 12" appliquéd Slicker Sue blocks. Nineteen 6" x 12" Mayflower blocks alternate with 6½" x 12½" rectangles.

Fabric Requirements: Divide amount needed by the number of fabrics and colors used.
   Blocks: 2½ yards for Slicker Sue, 5 yards for foundation, 3 yards for Mayflower blocks
   Backing: 5½ yards

Slicker Sue marches this way and that, carrying her ducky in a shower of color and spring posies.

Colorful backings create a rainbow reverse for That's Ducky.

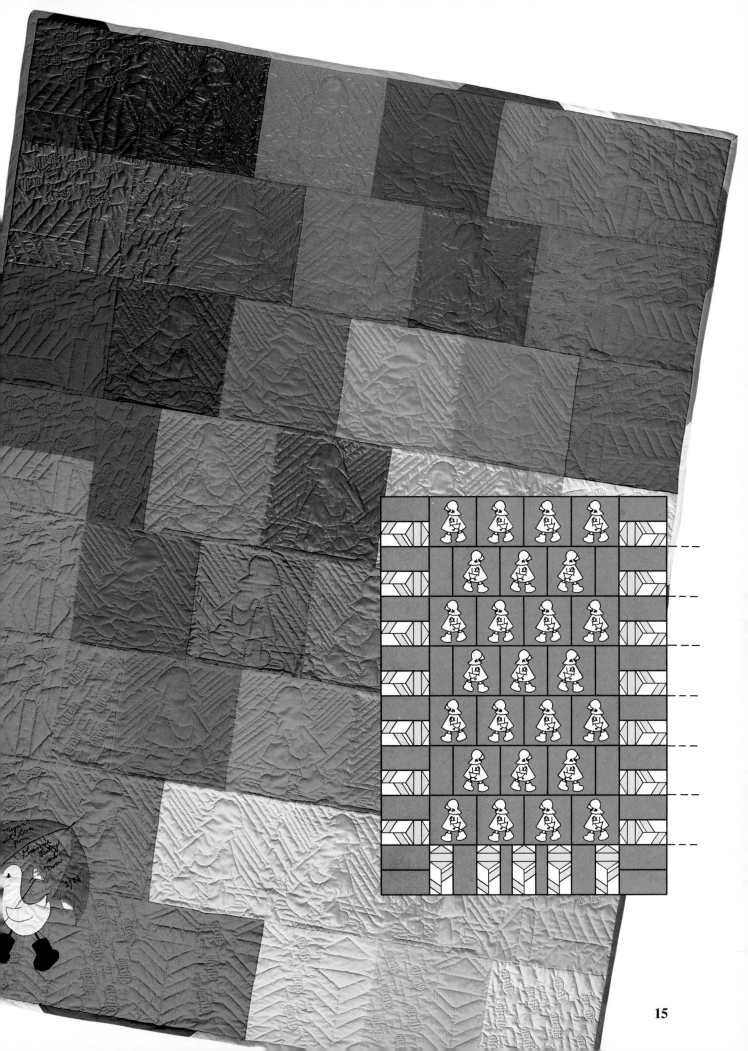

Use the grid drawing (Figure B) to enlarge Slicker Sue for the baby quilt. Cut foundation for center panel 22½″ x 30″. Center pattern pieces; then appliqué in place. The enlarged figure could also be made into a pillow doll.

That's Ducky Baby Quilt
Finished Size: 32″ x 40″
Perimeter: 140″
Center Panel: 22″ x 30″
Borders: 1″ wide and 4″ wide
Fabric Requirements: Divide amount needed by the number of fabrics and colors used.
  Center Panel: 1½ yards
  Border: 1 yard
  Backing: 1½ yards

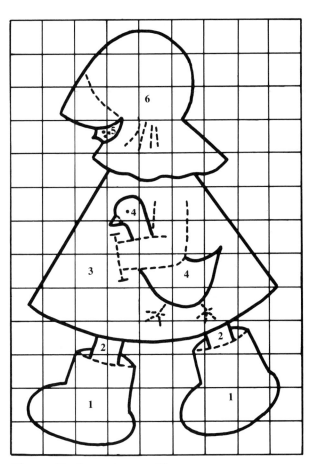

Figure B: 1 square = 2″.

An enlarged single Slicker Sue and her duck colorfully accent the baby's room.

Use the gridded design to make a Slicker Sue pillow to match the quilt.

Grandma Taught Us How

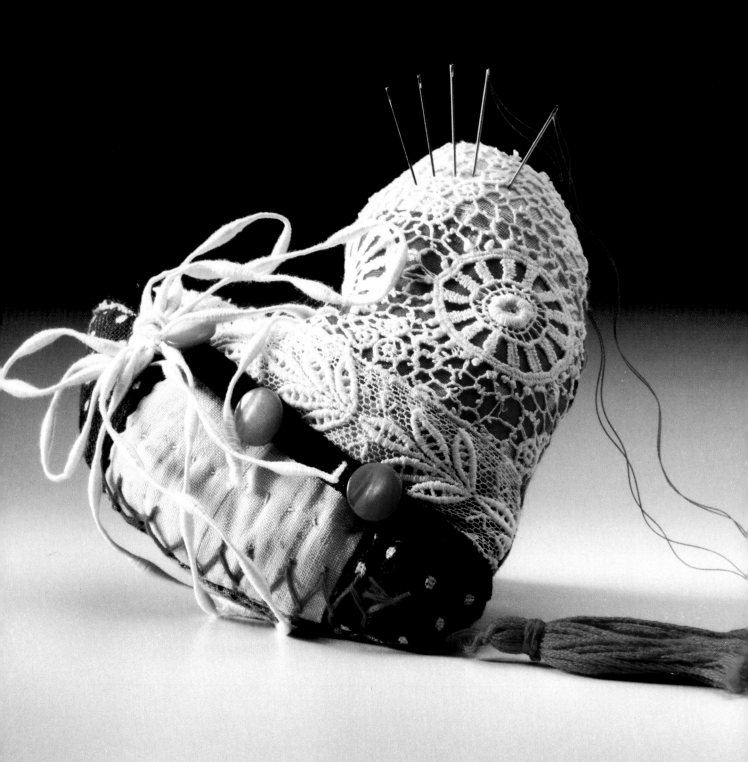

In many families, quilting skipped a generation. It was not our mothers, but our grandmothers or even our great-grandmothers, who stitched the bed covers. We owe our patchwork heritage to these creative foremothers. Today we may have plastic templates, abbreviated hoops for lap quilting, sewing machines that light up, and TV shows (instead of grandmas) that teach, but quilting is still the same craft. It's in the hands of a progressive people, all eager to continue the quilting experience and leave a quilting legacy.

THE GREAT QUILT CENSUS

Even before, and especially since, our country's bicentennial celebration, there has been a reawakening of our quilting heritage. Not only has this reawakening spurred us on to make quilts, but it has helped us realize the importance of cataloging and documenting our quilts. Many museums and volunteer groups across the country are involved in census programs that will add to our knowledge of fiber and textile history. Some states are even registering quilts made in that state between certain dates. Because of this present-day research, we are more conscious of two things: the need to sign, date, and verify the making of a quilt and the proper storage and care of a quilt. To take these two steps for posterity:

1. On a separate piece of muslin, type special messages, names, and dates or use indelible ink to write the information. Then attach the muslin to a back corner of the quilt. Or try hand embroidering initials and dates, to add a special personal touch to a quilt.

2. Remember, light is the worst enemy of our fiber art. Keep quilts away from strong sunlight and extremes of hot and cold. Don't store quilts in plastic bags or against paper or wood, since this will affect the fibers and promote staining. Some of our very fine, precious antique quilts just should not be laundered. When in doubt about care or handling of an old quilt, consult a textile authority.

Attending a quilt documentation day or a reading about quiltmaking of long ago, or viewing a collection of antique quilts, can be a moving experience. It corroborates what we do today, allowing us to see our stitchery as an extension of the handwork done over the centuries. As a result of my time spent in quiltmaking, I feel strong ties with today's quilters and the quilters of yesterday.

THE ALBUM QUILT

Discovering these old quilts awakens a desire to re-create the old patterns. One popular pattern is the Album block, sometimes called the Chimney Sweep block. Because of the

blank center rectangle, this block is an ideal place for signatures and sentiments. Quite often these blocks are stitched in calicoes that belonged to different people, which adds to the blocks' charm. A collection of these blocks with different signatures and fabrics becomes an irreplaceable friendship album.

Freedom Escape Album Quilt

For this particular album quilt, a special stamp was made. It was imprinted in the center of each rectangle with indelible ink. Then special signatures initialed each block. (Most office supply stores can make the rubber stamps for you. All that is required is clear, black artwork on white paper.)

This quilt is a great family project, a perfect Silver Anniversary gift. Try sending relatives the pieces in a package with precise instructions, or just send the pattern and let their return blocks be a surprise. If possible have the family members quilt the blocks or sections before returning them. (You're really putting lap quilting to use then!) After the squares are completed and returned, you can assemble the rows to finish the quilt.

My album quilt was made in a week-long quilt retreat where we shared calicoes brought from home. Each Album block is framed with a 1½″-wide, mitered muslin border. This makes the calicoes seem to float on the quilt surface. When blocks are set on point, as they are here, it is easier to lap-quilt in diagonal rows. But it is important to cut the backing so the fabric is on the straight of the grain when the block is

A special stamp was made for the names on this album quilt.

Signatures on these blocks recall happy days at the quilting retreat, Freedom Escape.

positioned in the quilt. That means the raw edges are cut on the bias. Calico from the blocks is used for the triangles on the ends of the diagonal rows to accent the perimeter of the quilt. Naturally, the quilt will find a home at the quilting retreat, Freedom Escape.

Freedom Escape Album Quilt
Finished Size: 63″ x 84″
Perimeter: 294″
Blocks: Eighteen 12″ Album blocks
Borders: 1½″-wide double muslin borders, ten side triangles, four corner triangles
Fabric Requirements:
    Blocks and border: 3 yards of calico, 3 yards of solids
    Backing: 5 yards

In the Hall of the Knights

A special print fabric was the inspiration for this wall hanging. Unusual colors for the Album blocks were chosen to match the print. Because this is a smaller quilt, it is in keeping to create an 8″ block. Since these blocks are set on point, lap-quilt diagonal rows instead of individual blocks.

In the Hall of the Knights
Finished Size: 45¼″ x 45¼″
Perimeter: 181″
Blocks: Nine 8″ Album blocks, sixteen print blocks
Borders: Twelve side triangles and four corner triangles
Fabric Requirements:
    Album blocks: 1 yard (divide by number of fabrics used)
    Print: 1 yard
    Solid: 1 yard
    Backing: 1½ yards

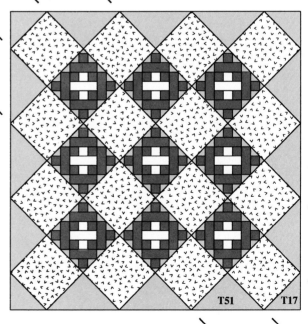

In the Hall of the Knights *is an updated, smaller version of the Album block, inspired by a special floral fabric.*

A sentimental keepsake quilt presents an Album quilt block with a new slant.

For Ellen: Remember Me

Although separated by many miles today, memories of a lifelong friendship are recalled and stitched in the muted, old-fashioned fabrics of this album quilt.

For Ellen: Remember Me
Finished Size: 68″ x 89¼″
Perimeter: 314½″

Blocks: Eighteen 12″ Album blocks
Borders: 3″ x 12″ lattice and 3″ square inserts, ten side triangles, and four corner triangles
Fabric Requirements:
  Blocks and sawtooth edging: 2 yards of remnants
  Triangles and inserts: 2 yards
  Lattice borders: 1 yard
  Backing: 5 yards

T20

T48

UPDATED CLASSICS

Grandma taught us how to make these traditional patterns, but we've made slight changes to update the classic designs. Here the *Jewelry Box* quilt reminds us of Jacob's Ladder, and the *Buzz Saw* quilt suggests a Sawtooth Star pattern gone askew.

Swirling triangles suggest a saw's cutting blades.

Jewelry Box
Finished Size: 78″ x 94″
Perimeter: 344″
Blocks: Twenty 16″ blocks
Borders: 2″-wide inside border, 5″-wide outside border
Fabric Requirements: Divide amount needed by the number of fabrics and colors used.
  Blocks: Muslin, 3 yards; scraps, 3 yards
Borders: 2½ yards each of two colors (needed for length)
Backing: 6 yards

Buzz Saw
Finished Size: 80″ x 96″
Perimeter: 352″
Blocks: Sixty 8″ Buzz Saw blocks, sixty 8½″ solid squares
Borders: Sawtooth edging
Fabric Requirements: Divide amount needed by the number of fabrics and colors used.
  Blocks: 6 yards
  Border: 2 yards
  Backing: 5½ yards

Calicoes galore prance across the muslin surface in a gay, vivid quilt.

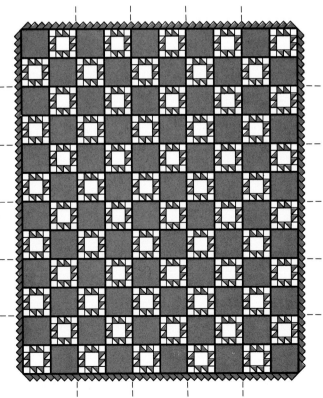

The Homestead

Update another all-time favorite by creating mirror images framed in navy blue. The chimney and border accents are a red plaid. A pieced border highlights the perimeter of this quilt. The lap quilting is broken down into 12 sections, including the offset borders. Bright red binding sets off the finished edges.

To create the 24 blocks needed (12 mirror images), follow these instructions for cutting and piecing (Figure A).

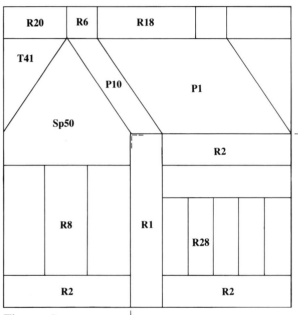

Figure A

1. P1 template (roof). Cut 12 dark; reverse; cut 12 light.

2. P10 (angle connector). Cut 12 dark; reverse; cut 12 light.

3. T41 (sky triangle). Cut 12 sets of dark (mirror images) and 12 sets of light.

4. Sp50 (gable). Cut 12 dark and 12 light.

5. R2. Cut 48 dark and 48 light.

6. R1. Cut 12 dark and 12 light.

A classic pattern takes a new turn with a mirror-image setting and plaid accents.

Rather than cutting individual pieces for these templates, take advantage of quick piecing. Sew strips together and then cut to form the sections of the sky and windows.

7. Sky and chimney sections. Cut two dark strips and two light strips, each 30″ long and the width of template R20. Cut two dark strips and two light, each 30″ long and the width of R6.

Cut one dark strip and one light strip, each 30″ long and the width of R18.

Starting with a dark color, sew strips together in this order: R20 + R6 + R18 + R6 + R20, alternating colors. Starting with a light strip, sew bands together, alternating colors and following the same order. Cut 12 sections of light sky and 12 dark the width of R18.

8. Section of house and two windows. Cut five dark strips and five light strips, each 54″ long and the width of R28. Beginning with a light strip, sew five strips together, alternating colors. Beginning with a dark strip, sew the remaining five strips together, alternating colors. Cut 12 sections of light windows and 12 dark windows the width of R28.

9. Large window and side of the house. Cut three dark strips and three light strips, each 72″ long and the width of R8. Beginning with a light strip, sew three strips together, alternating colors. Beginning with a dark strip, sew the remaining three strips together, alternating colors. Cut 12 sections of light windows and 12 dark windows the width of R8.

To complete the Homestead block, sew P1 and Sp50 to the diagonal piece P10. Then attach the triangle sky pieces T41. Attach the row with the chimneys. Sew the R8 window section and the R2 together and add to Sp50. Complete the section with the small windows by adding rectangles R2 and R1. Attach this section with a free-floating seam at right angle.

A pieced border is added to the outside in ten sections. The square, set on point, is framed by alternating dark and light trapezoids. Small triangles offset the square to form the trapezoid when the final connection is made for lap quilting. When piecing, sew up to the ¼″ mark; stop and backstitch to create free-floating seams.

The Homestead

Finished Size: 70″ x 101″

Perimeter: 342″

Blocks: Twenty-four 14″ blocks (12 mirror image)

Borders: 2″-wide sashing, 2″-wide pieced border

Fabric Requirements:

Blocks: 2 yards of white, 2 yards of blue

Border and chimney: 1 yard of red

Sashing: 2 yards

Backing: 6 yards

Pieced, lap-quilted, just waiting to be joined—these twelve sections of The Homestead *quilt already include the sashing and borders.*

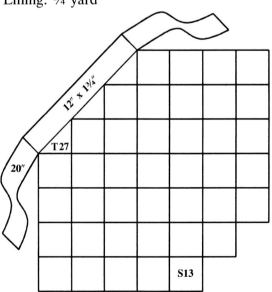

Pastel squares make a pretty cover-up.

A Square Meal

For your own homestead make this simple cover-up in an array of pastel colors. Use the pieced apron as a pattern to cut out the lining. With right sides together, sew a ¼″ seam around the sides and bottom. Invert at the open waistband area; then attach a waistband with ties. If you use an overlock machine, there's no need to line the apron.

A Square Meal Apron
Finished Size: 30″ x 20″
Fabric Requirements: Assorted calico remnants
    Lining: ¾ yard

An eagle emerges in this 22" x 32" collage.

CRAZY PATCH UPDATE

People associate Crazy Patch with their grandmothers' Victorian quilts. In those days people dressed in silks and velvets, so the remnants were naturally sewn into Crazy Patch throws. Those silky throws were decorative and complemented the furnishings of the times.

If you are the fortunate owner of one of these elaborate quilts, you might consider donating it to a museum in the area where it was made. It would be a great contribution and could even reveal a bit of that area's history. If you have a square that never made it into a quilt, it could be framed professionally, to protect it from impending moisture. (Be sure the framers use acid-free paper and mat board.)

The intricate handwork and jewel-like fabrics of the top are still appreciated, but you can update Crazy Patch. All those outdated and over-and-under-sized men's ties you have been hesitant to throw away can actually be put to use in creating new Crazy Patch. The ties can take on new character in evening bags. They can be sewn together with the narrow ends at the top to make a skirt. Or they can be used as accents on jacket lapels and cummerbunds.

The image of an eagle seen in a floor mat at a U.S. Post Office was the inspiration for a silhouette Crazy Patch Eagle design. The outline of the eagle was positioned and traced on foundation material. The odd-shaped pieces of material were attached to the base fabric. (The colors change when crossing from the figure to the background material.) Be certain that the tie fabric is clean (devoid of chicken soup!), pressed, and cut into similar-sized pieces with interesting angles. Attach random pieces using the sew-and-flip method, or position the piece, pin it in place, and hand appliqué. Embroidery stitches in dark thread around the eagle and in light blue for the sky help to distinguish the figure.

A Crazy Patch square takes to the wall to become an heirloom picture.

Elegance abounds in this muted Crazy Crane *design.*

Continual Crazy Patch with a silhouette tucked inside is exemplified in the *Crazy Crane* wall piece. The elegant crane emerges in shades of white and ecru against a putty background. Eight rectangular panels depict the random Crazy Patch design embellished with elaborate hand embroidery and dangling trinkets. Using the eagle and the crane as inspiration, unlock your imagination and create your own Crazy Patch picture.

Breaking the Rules

O ver the years we quilters have developed certain standards in quiltmaking that have become accepted as unwritten laws, among them: hand quilting, using geometric templates that have seams included, using only 100% cotton fabric, and never using any checks or plaids. But I propose that breaking these rules can lead to discovery and unexpected rewards.

MACHINE QUILTING

Please don't be afraid to try machine quilting. Our machine piecework today has allowed us to create a mountain of quilt tops that are just waiting to be quilted. Machine quilting with a strong lock stitch saves us time and allows us to quilt more quilts. When you think about it—won't we stay just as warm under a machine-quilted quilt? Of course!

Machine quilting a full-size, layered quilt is very difficult because of the amount of fabric you must handle. Machine quilting in sections is a logical solution to the problem. These sections can be blocks or rows, but remember to leave ½" free at outside connecting edges. This is just as important as in hand quilting. When machine quilting, never try to emulate hand quilting; instead, take advantage of your sewing machine's capabilities. I break machine quilting into two categories:

1. Contrary Machine Quilting: With feed dogs up as in normal sewing, use a walking or even-feed foot to create uniform stitches. Stitch a continuous pattern that does not follow the lines of the piecework. (Stitches that echo the line of piecing create bulk at the intersections, and many starts and stops result in lots of loose threads.) Match the bobbin and top thread to the quilt backing and be sure to backstitch at the start and finish. Consider using a transparent thread on top (not on the bobbin). You might also try using a wide zigzag stitch directly on top of the piecework in a contrasting thread.

2. Meandering, Loitering, or Free-Motion Quilting: For this technique, you should drop the feed dogs and sew a continuous quilting line. First, anchor the layers of fabric with a narrow hoop. Place the inside smaller ring on top of the fabric and the larger ring underneath against the machine. Pull the bobbin thread to the surface and take several stitches in one place before beginning the meandering process. With feed dogs dropped, determine the stitch length by moving and turning the material inside the hoop. Develop your own fun patterns. To practice and build up confidence in machine quilting, simply follow a printed fabric design and let yourself go on the machine! End your quilting the same way you began—stop, sew in place, and clip off threads.

The *NBC* and *Spool Twist* quilts are examples of machine quilting.

CHECK IT OUT

Quilters rarely use gingham fabric for piecing for this reason: when the checks are cut and then resewn they don't match, and this creates confusion. The secret to using this fabric successfully is to isolate the checks. Look for odd-size checked fabric that can coordinate in color, but contrast in size.

In the two baby quilts, *Tie Dog* and *Bow Cat,* I did just that. I broke the rules and used gingham fabric, because it has always been associated with babies. But I placed the checks strategically so that they didn't have to match.

Tie Dog and Bow Cat

Gingham cats and dogs decorate two separate baby quilts in a fifteen-block arrangement of 12″ squares. The pieced animal blocks alternate with the tie and the bow blocks.

When piecing the animal blocks, sew just up to the ¼″ mark for the tail of the cat and dog, to create a free-floating seam. To make the bias ruffle that softens the outside of each quilt, cut one yard of fabric into a bias strip 6½″ wide and 288″ long.

The animal mobile is an extra dividend, made to match the *Bow Cat* and *Tie Dog* quilts. Sew the two sides of each figure together, leaving a small section unstitched for turning. Turn the figures right side out and then stuff them with polyester filling. Whipstitch the opening closed. Accent the neckline of each animal with ribbon or bias strips.

The matching swinging dog and cat mobile will entertain the baby for hours.

The secret to using checks is to isolate them, as in our adorable baby quilts, Tie Dog *and* Bow Cat.

Cut two lattice boards 18″ long. To allow for gathers, cut the fabric to cover the boards twice as long as the board and slightly wider. Sew the fabric into a tube, leaving one end open; turn. Slip the board inside the fabric tube, gathering the fabric to fit the board. Staple the fabric in place at both ends of each board. Connect the two boards with a swivel pin. Hang the hearts and animals with narrow satin ribbon and just watch the grins appear on little faces!

Tie Dog

Finished Size: 36″ x 60″

Perimeter: 192″

Blocks: Three 12″ Tie Dog blocks, twelve 12″ Tie blocks

Fabric Requirements: Divide amount needed by the number of fabrics and colors used.

Blocks: 2½ yards

Backing: 1¾ yards

Ruffle: 1 yard

Bow Cat

Finished Size: 36″ x 60″

Perimeter: 192″

Blocks: Three 12″ Bow Cat blocks, twelve 12″ Bow blocks

Fabric Requirements: Divide amount needed by the number of fabrics and colors used.

Blocks: 2½ yards

Backing: 1¾ yards

Ruffle: 1 yard

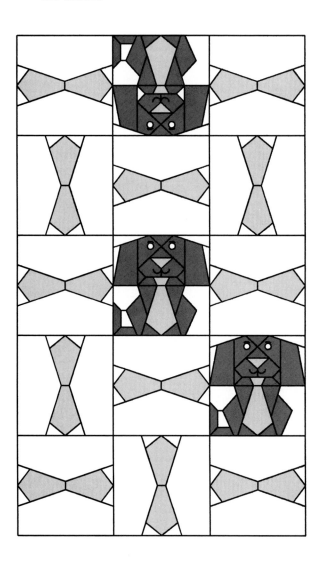

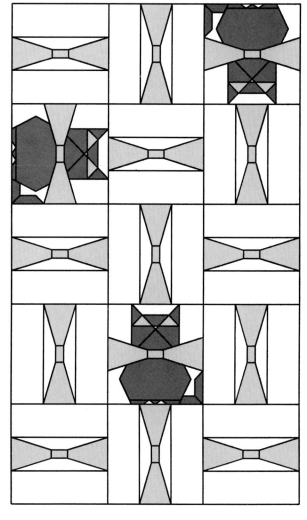

The Best-Dressed Cat In Town

Can you find the Bow Cat lost in this array of colorful bow tie blocks? This is a great scrap quilt idea, full of vim and vigor! Four colorful ties make up each 12″ block. Sew four 12″ blocks together and then lap-quilt the larger blocks. After quilting and assembling all the Bow Tie blocks and the Bow Cat block, use the sew-and-extend method to add the navy blue border and sawtooth edging. Stack the fabrics, aligning raw edges, as follows: backing of border, right side up; the quilt, right side up; border top, wrong side up; and finally border batting. Sew all four layers together. Fold back the two pieces of border fabric and the batting and baste them together. Quilt the border, but leave ½″ around the outside of the border free to attach the sawtooth edges of the triangles.

Use the Bow Cat block to make a coordinating pillow for *The Best-Dressed Cat in Town*.

The Best-Dressed Cat in Town

Finished Size: 106″ x 82″
Perimeter: 376″
Blocks: Forty-seven 12″ Bow Tie blocks, one 12″ Bow Cat block
Borders: 5″ border plus sawtooth edging
Fabric Requirements: Divide amount needed by the number of fabrics and colors used.
   Blocks: 3 yards of muslin, 4 yards of scraps
   Backing: 6 yards
   Border: 3 yards
   Sawtooth edging: 2 yards of scraps

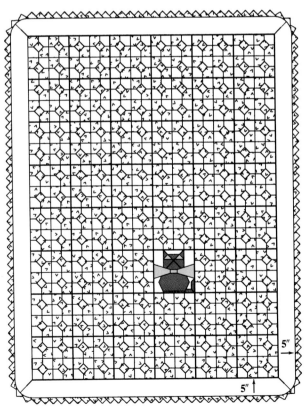

MAKING PLAIDS WORK

A madras plaid quilt—what madness to even consider such a thing! But Jill Moore, my sister, had a collection of leftover madras and wanted a quilt. After surveying our pattern options, we discovered the perfect one for *Madras Madness*—a pineapple pattern. Since we cut the madras on the bias and sewed the strips at an angle, they sit in the block on the straight of the grain, giving the block stability. Colors and plaid lines converge, creating a kaleidoscope of color. Rather than sewing each strip onto a marked muslin foundation, Jill used twelve paper blueprints as a foundation.

She then sewed the four center triangles together to form a square and pinned the square in place on the paper. With the paper as a base,

she sewed and flipped the 1"-wide strips around the center square, alternating four solid and four madras strips. Do shorten the stitch length on the machine when sewing on paper, so that the paper will easily pull away from the fabric after stitching. End with the large corner triangles (T24), alternating solid and madras.

To make the turquoise and fuchsia border, sew 1½"-wide strips together, alternating colors. Sew nineteen strips together to form a piece 21" long and 19½" wide. Then sew twenty-two strips together to form a piece 28" long and 22½" wide. Cut both pieces apart every 3½" at a right angle to the strips. Sew the bands with twenty-two strips to the corner blocks and miter the corners. Sew the bands with the nineteen strips to the remaining blocks. Add borders to the back of blocks to create a reversible quilt.

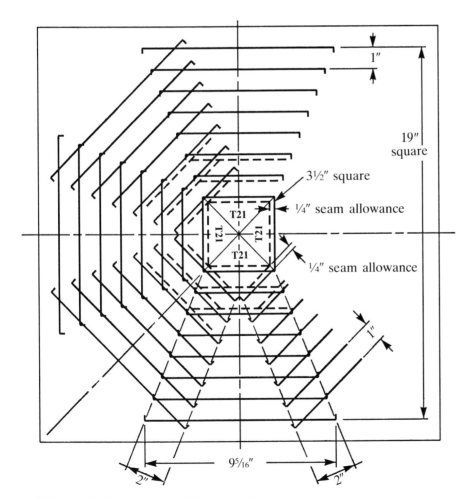

Figure A
Draw a diagram for a 19" - square block, using Figure A as a reference. Have 12 copies made of it at a blueprinters. (It doesn't cost much.) In the center of the block, draw the 3" square made up of four triangles. Draw the lines showing where to add the 1"-wide strips. The strips are added to the square from the center outward. Your material can be sewn directly onto the 12 paper blocks.

Madras finds a home in this pineapple design.

Lap-quilt the individual blocks. Then assemble the blocks, positioning the large madras triangles next to the large solid triangles. This creates a stunning secondary pattern. Finally, bind the quilt with madras fabric.

Madras Madness
Finished Size: 63″ x 82″
Perimeter: 290″
Blocks: Twelve 19″ Pineapple blocks
Borders: 3″ pieced border
Fabric Requirements:
    Madras remnants— 3 yards
    Fuchsia—2 yards
    Turquoise—2 yards
    Backing—5 yards

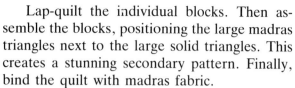

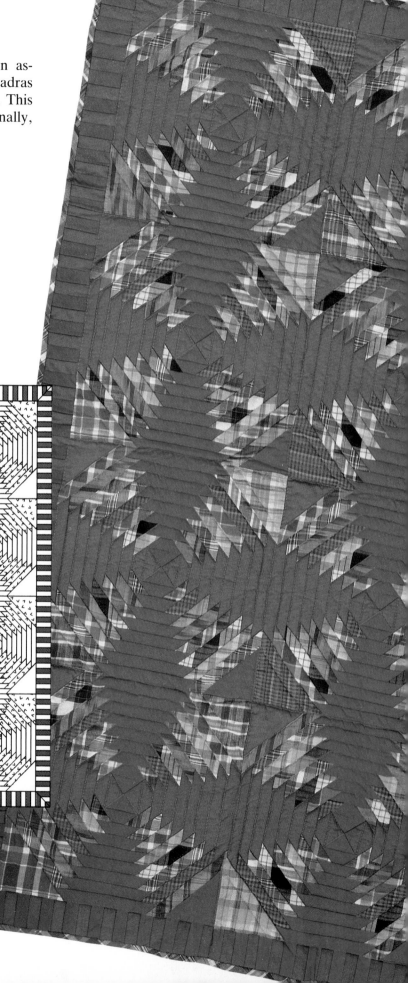

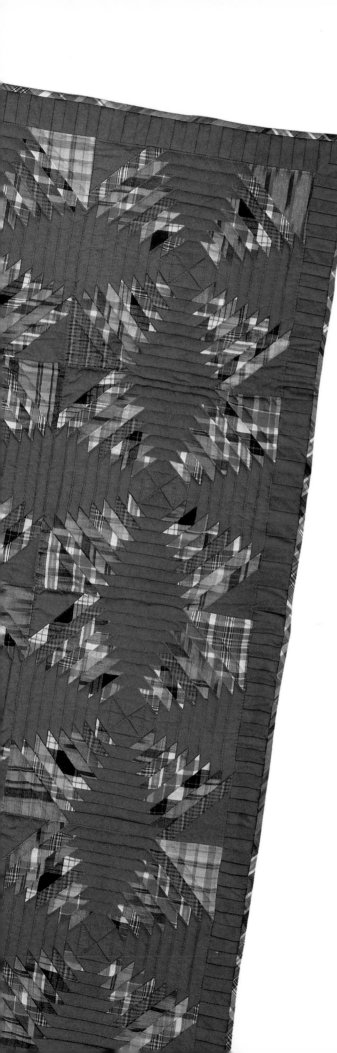

Use the slip-and-slide bargello technique to create one-of-a-kind clothing designs.

BARGELLO PATCHFUN

Forget geometric templates when you create a slip-and-slide bargello quilt or garment. This design is reminiscent of decorative needlepoint. You can make it in miniature or stitch a large pieced cloth. Strips of fabric are cut, sewn together, and recut, creating rows of colorful rectangles. This technique differs from Seminole patchwork because, in that technique, angles are introduced in a second cut.

A Nice Bargello Centerpiece *adds a touch of modern art to the home.*

The scale of your design should be determined by your garment or quilt. A 2½″ cut works well for garments. Measure the length and divide by the desired width of the strip to figure how many strips are needed. For instance, for a 20″ vest back using a 2″-wide strip, you will need to cut ten pieces, each 2½″ wide. (Allow ½″ for two ¼″ seams.)

The possibilities for designs with the variegated bands are endless. The colors can be a full seam apart (Figure A) or a half seam apart (Figure B) to vary the flamestitch design. As bands shift you will need a seam ripper, since some colors will need to be removed from one end and resewn to the opposite end. This reworking of the bands is an accepted part of the technique.

Bands can be cut apart and separated by a contrasting strip of fabric. Or the bands can be resewn to form a diamond with contrasting strips in between (Figure C). Rather than making even strips in the first cut, you could cut uneven strips (Figure D) to create an asymmetrical look as shown in the *NBC Quilt*.

The second cut for this quilt also introduces various widths. Cut one strip 3″ wide; four 2½″

Figure A

Figure B

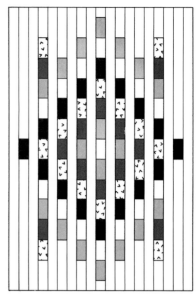

Figure C

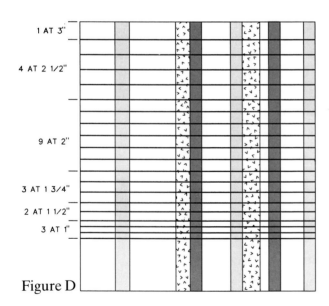

Figure D

1 AT 3″

4 AT 2 1/2″

9 AT 2″

3 AT 1 3/4″

2 AT 1 1/2″

3 AT 1″

wide; nine 2″ wide; three 1¾″ wide; two 1½″ wide and three 1″ wide.

NBC Quilt
Finished Size: 36″ x 40″
Perimeter: 152″
Borders: 1½″ wide

Fabric Requirements:
   Top and border: Narrow strips of seven bright colors, cut 2″ to 3″ wide. Alternate and sew with white strips, cut 6″ to 8″.
   Backing: 1½ yards

BARGELLO PATCHFUN

If you are ready to slip-and-slide,
follow these steps.

1. Planning the Design. Use colored construction paper to test your design and create the desired effect. Decide on the color range—four to six colors with an accent color are best. Place a light color next to the darkest color.

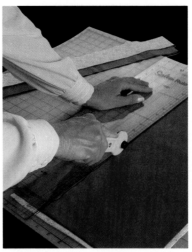

2. Making the First Cut. After determining the width of your strips, use a rotary cutter (a must for a bargello project) to cut the fabric strips on the crosswise fold of the fabric.

3. Sewing Your Colored Strips Together. This forms your own striped fabric. Press all the seams in the same direction.

4. Making the Second Cut. Cut apart at a right angle the fabric you just created. This determines the width of the resewn variegated bands. Don't cut the fabric the same width as the original cut unless you want squares. (A 1½″ cut works well here.)

5. Sewing Bands Together. Sew these variegated bands directly to one another, right sides facing, raw edges aligned, and seams in a downward direction or . . .

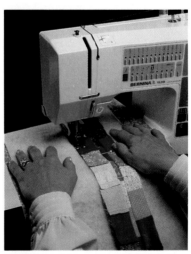

Use a walking or even-feed foot and sew bands directly onto a foundation or the actual lining of a garment. Cut the foundation and batting at least ½″ longer on each end than the variegated bands. Position center band in place. Attach the next bands to the center band, alternating sides. Sew from top to bottom.

Chinese Lanterns *is a template-free wool quilt, based on bands of fabric.*

Chinese Lanterns

My bargello quilt, *Chinese Lanterns,* breaks all kinds of rules. Since it is a bargello quilt it requires no templates or hand quilting. It is also made of wool, which is rarely used for quilting. Wool does not adapt well to tiny 45°-angle templates nor to a lot of hand quilting, due to its depth and texture. Keeping those characteristics in mind, however, we can alter our quilt.

Create two variations of striped fabric. For the first striped fabric, cut 12½″-wide strips across the 60″ widths of a dark, a bright, and a light fabric. Sew these strips together on the 60″ edges to form a multicolored band. Repeat these steps twice more. Then sew the three bands together on the 60″ edges to make a 108″ section.

For the variation of the band, cut across the widths of all three fabrics at 18½″ and 6½″. Sew these strips together on the 60″ edges, alternating wide and narrow strips and colors, until band measures 90″.

Now, at a right angle, cut across the strips of both bands at 3½″ intervals. (You need seven rows of the first striped band and 14 rows of the variation.)

Cut a backing and a batting 2″ longer at each end than the desired length of your top, to allow for any take-up. Lay the batting on top of the backing and locate the vertical center. Pin the center 3½″-wide strip in place. Tightly roll the sides of the quilt and transport to the ma-

chine. Align the next band with the center band, right sides facing and raw edges matching. Sew in place, using a walking foot and a bobbin thread that matches the quilt backing. As you attach each strip, always sew from the same direction. The sew-and-flip method may be awkward because of bulk, but keep telling yourself that it will all be done in one fell swoop—sewing and quilting.

Sew a ruffle to all four sides to finish the quilt. Cut two yards of fabric into bias strips 16½″ wide and 459″ long.

Chinese Lanterns
Finished Size: 63″ x 90″
Perimeter: 306″ (without ruffle)
Fabric Requirements:
  Top, 60″-wide fabrics: Dark, 2 yards; bright, 2 yards; light, 2 yards
  Backing: 4½ yards
  Ruffle: 2 yards

Firebird

A bargello design to boggle the mind! Proceed with caution . . . serious piecing instructions ahead! Just as a road sign indicates a hairpin curve or a dangerous intersection, you need to be alerted to the awesome task of developing this wall piece. If you are one of the quilters who find the glory in the process of quiltmaking as well as the end product, then revel in this design, a product of our Year Quilt Class. Joan Pierro, a most patient quilter, found her original inspiration for *Firebird* in a needlepoint design book.

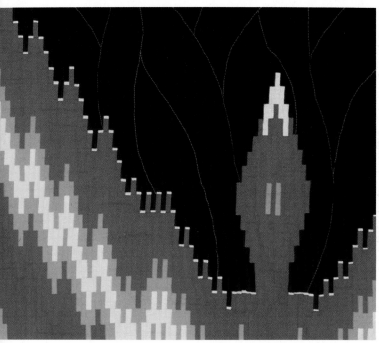

Take a closer look at the tiny pieces in Firebird.

To piece the bird, you need four colors of fabric, plus black fabric for the background. Cut the strips on the crosswise grain 2″ wide. Sew the strips together, repeating the color sequence 1, 2, 3, 4. Cut this fabric vertically into ¾″-wide strips. Also cut various lengths of ¾″-wide strips of black fabric. A total of 16 yards of these black strips is needed for the background, with the longest black piece measuring 24″.

Following the grid, slip-and-slide your strips to create the Firebird design. In the body of the bird, it will be necessary to rip out colors and resew them to obtain the desired effect. Notice the yellow accents at the wing tips. When the colored strips are aligned, sew black strips to them to complete the background. Once all the strips are complete, sew them to one another.

For the 2″-wide border, sew 1″-wide strips of each of the four colors together.

Enlarging this design could produce a bargello *Firebird* to cover a bed. That would require starting with 4″-wide bands instead of 2″ bands, and the second cut would be 1½″ instead of ¾″. You could also alter the outside border to accommodate the size of your bed.

Firebird
Finished Size: 58″ x 70″
Perimeter: 256″
Fabric Requirements:
   Top and borders: 2 yards each of four colors
   Backing: 5 yards

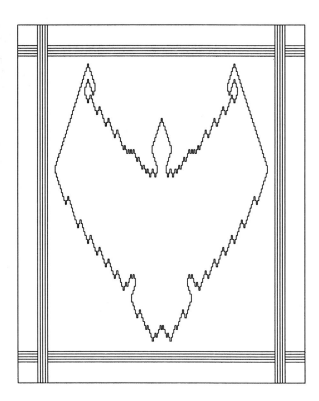

Firebird *radiates warmth and excitement.*

Spooling Around

The spool is one of the oldest tools in textile history and basic to all forms of spinning. My initial encounter with the spool shape led to my *Spinning Spools* sampler in *More Lap Quilting*. Taking the essence of that design, the two triangles and the trapezoid that form a square, I repositioned the squares at various angles and formed new blocks. "Spooling around" with shapes may completely erase any suggestion of the original design, but it is a good way to begin expanding a block.

THE EXPANDING SPOOL

New looks for a familiar block can also be created just by changing where the light and dark areas fall within the block. The first set of squares illustrates the look of light triangles and dark trapezoids in one block (Figure A). The second set is just reversed (Figure B). The trapezoids are light, and the triangles are dark. A third option combines an equal number of light and dark triangles and light and dark trapezoids (Figure C). The difference in the blocks is created by juggling the units.

Another expand-a-block idea is elongating a square into a rectangle. When this is done with the spool block, an angled spool emerges (Figure D). Adding new lines can also change the look of your block, but remember, each line represents a seam and a new template (Figure E). Be cautious of too many angles radiating from one area or skinny points that fade away, since they mean multiple seam allowances. Eliminating lines could simplify your design (Figure F). Or try introducing a curve to alter the shape (Figure G).

By introducing 60° and 45° angles, diamond shapes create new spool angles. The spool becomes short and fat or gets long and skinny. These diamonds have possibilities as Tumbling Block or star designs (Figure H).

A mathematician told me that this one 16-patch spool block has 4,294,967,283 combinations. I'll never discover all of them, but this is why quilters love patchwork.

Figure A: Light triangles and dark trapezoids

Figure B: Dark triangles and light trapezoids

Figure C: An equal number of light and dark triangles and light and dark trapezoids

Figure D: Elongating

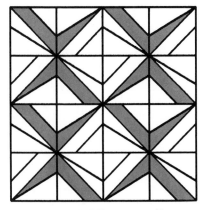

Figure E: Adding new lines

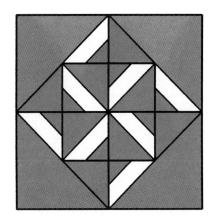

Figure F: Eliminating lines

Figure G: Adding a curve

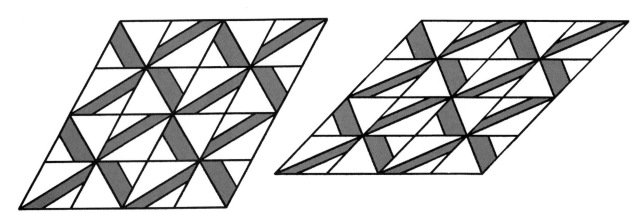

Figure H: Adding angles

A no-sew no-quilt project combines the geometric variations of the Spool block.

Painless Patchwork Project

This sampler vividly demonstrates a variety of designs discovered by expanding a spool block motif. What makes the project unique is that it is done without sewing or quilting. What a great opportunity to create instant patchwork or test colors and fabrics!

Using a pencil, draw each block full-size on the non-shiny side of freezer paper. Code each template with the grain line and color. After cutting out the templates (a rotary cutter helps here), lightly press them, shiny side down, onto the back of your fabrics. Trim the excess fabric around the paper template.

Mark the position of the 12″ squares, sashing, and small spool inserts on a piece of foam board, mat board, or strong flat cardboard.

Think of the fabric templates as a puzzle. Glue each piece in place and you are done! It's a quick and easy project, emitting the warmth of glowing fabric!

Patchwork Project (stitched version)
Finished Size: 48″ x 48″
Perimeter: 192″
Sampler blocks: Nine 12″ blocks

1. Wooden Thangs   5. Spools
2. Spool Twist   6. Hither & Yon
3. Mary Lee We   7. Spyrogyro
   Roll Along   8. Secret Drawer
4. Spinning Spools   9. Spool Spin-Off

Borders: ½″-wide blue border; 3″-wide print borders and sashing with sixteen 3″ spool blocks

*For the stitched version
of my sampler, I substituted the
Spinning Spools block for the Apple Core design.*

Fabric Requirements: Divide amount needed
   by the number of fabrics and colors used.
  Blocks: 2 yards of coordinated fabrics
  Borders and sashing: 1½ yards
  Backing: 2 yards

Spool Twist

Spool Twist is one of the patterns in the *Painless Patchwork Project* that was expanded from the original Spool block. Over a long period of time I pigeonholed this collection of coordinated colors, knowing full well that they would find a home in a quilt some day. As I pieced each 6″ square, I matched the fabric of one triangle and one trapezoid, but the fabrics varied from block to block. I kept the accent fabric, used in the figure that formed the pin-wheel, consistent throughout the quilt. Some squares are dark and some are light so that the pattern has a radiating effect. The triangles in the pieced border create a secondary design.

Spool Twist is unique in that the separate blocks were both hand- and machine-quilted. I basted with lots of straight pins and hand-quilted a minimum, but identical, amount on each 6″ square (Figure I). Be careful toting these blocks around; family members won't care for wandering pins in the carpet! After completing the hand quilting, you can easily machine-quilt a continuous pattern. No basting threads or pins are needed because of the hand quilting. Use a walking or even-feed foot on the machine. Start quilting at a corner. Stitch diagonally through the center to the web motif. Machine-quilt the rows of the web. Quilt a meandering loop motif in the border.

Spool Twist
Finished Size: 88″ x 72″
Perimeter: 320″
Blocks: Twenty 12″ Spool Twist blocks
Borders: 2″-wide border
Fabric Requirements: Divide amount needed by the number of fabrics and colors used.
   Blocks: 6 yards of coordinated scraps
   Backing: 5 yards

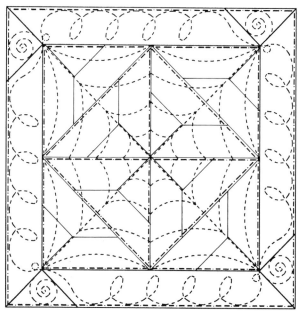

A combination of hand and machine quilting highlight Spool Twist.

Figure I
Machine quilting - - -   Hand quilting ― ― · ― ·

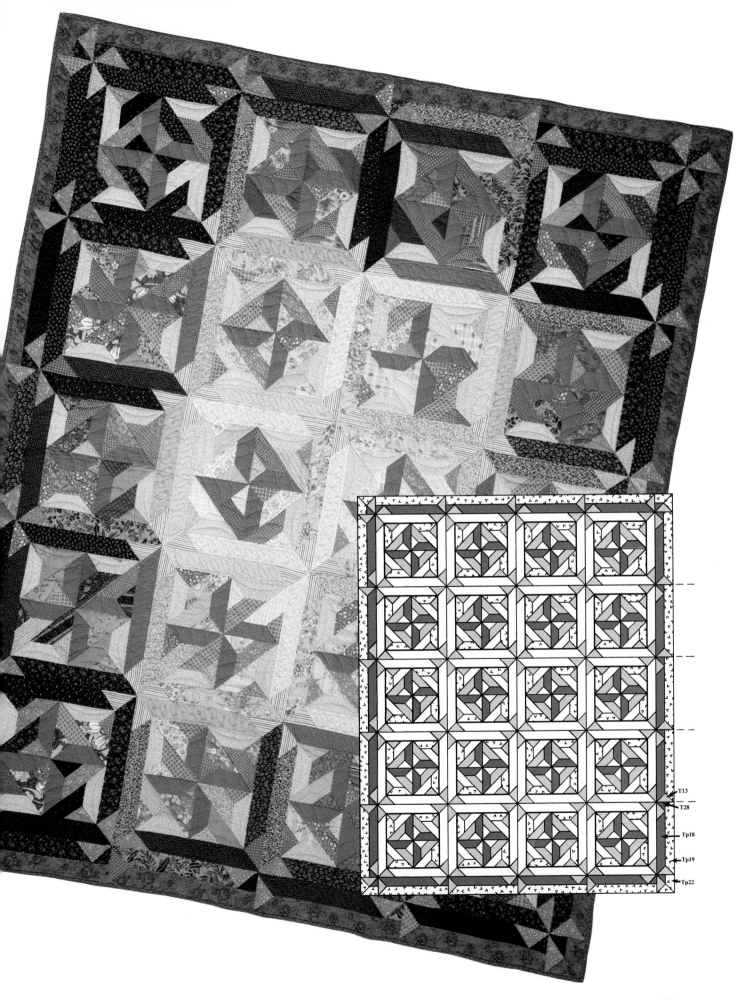

T13
T28
Tp18
Tp19
Tp22

Pillow Talk

Using four 12″ blocks of the Spool Twist pattern, Marilou Kimble has created a handsome pillow that will help make any home scene cozy. The patchwork pulls around to the back, completely covering the pillow form. Our 24″ Spool Twist block formed a 17″ pillow. If you use an 18″ block it will cover a 13″ pillow.

To make the pillow, quilt the layers of a pieced top. Fold the quilted block in half with the right sides together and stitch across each end with a ¼″ seam, backstitching to secure.

Fold the side seams together so that an interrupted seam connects the side, leaving a 10″ center opening (Figure J). (This technique is identical to the Cathedral Window quilt method.) Sew a piece of Velcro (¼″ wide x 10″ long) to each side of the opening. Turn the block right side out. Insert a pillow form.

A garden of geometric flowers grows on a soft quilt surface.

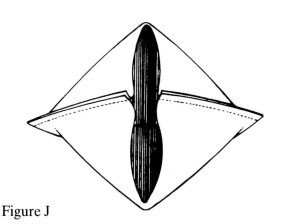

Figure J

A WORLD OF POSSIBILITIES

Creativity appears in everyday signs. The graphic art we see day in and day out abounds with potential quilt designs. As quilters we can expand the geometric designs from bank trademarks, club banners, or commercial logos. We can experiment with the designs, changing the sizes, the shapes, and the colors to suit our templates and our blocks. If we look at the names of our foremothers' quilting blocks we can see that they were also influenced by what

surround the blocks with square insets at the corner intersections.

Pretty Posy

Finished Size: 65″ x 94⅝″

Perimeter: 319¼″

Blocks: Eight 12″ Pretty Posy blocks, six side triangles, four corner triangles

Borders: 2″-wide border with a 1″ mitered border around each block

Fabric Requirements: Divide amount needed by the number of fabrics and colors used.

   Blocks: 2 yards

   Triangles: 2½ yards

   Borders: 2½ yards

   Backing: 6 yards

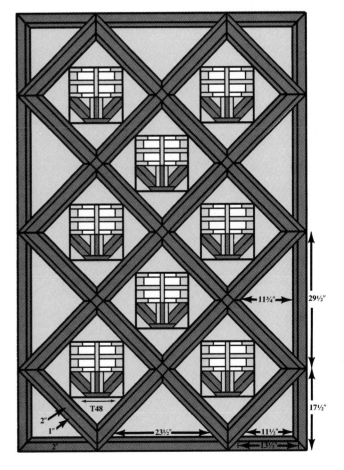

they saw around them—nature, log cabins, political figures.

Pretty Posy

I designed the block Pretty Posy after looking at the flower logo on my sewing machine. That sweet little flower takes on a new character once it decorates a quilt top.

The blocks, set in a field of yellow and framed by triangles, create a soft and feminine air in the *Pretty Posy* quilt. Mitered borders

Introducing a gentle curve to a rectangle results in a quilt with straight sides and wavy top and bottom.

Assorted fabrics gathered from friends come together in The Charming Wave *tablecloth.*

The Wave

By spooling around with the two long sides of a simple rectangle, we can develop a new shape. The long sides are curved, forming a tilted template. Since the top and bottom of the quilt are wavy, lap quilting is done in vertical rows. The template can be cut the same for each piece, or it can be flipped every other row to create a more distinct waving pattern as in *The Charming Wave* tablecloth.

The Wave
Finished Size: 114″ x 96″
Perimeter: 420″
Rectangles: One template
Fabric Requirements: Divide amount needed
    by the number of fabrics and colors used.
  Rectangles: 9 yards
  Backing: 7 yards

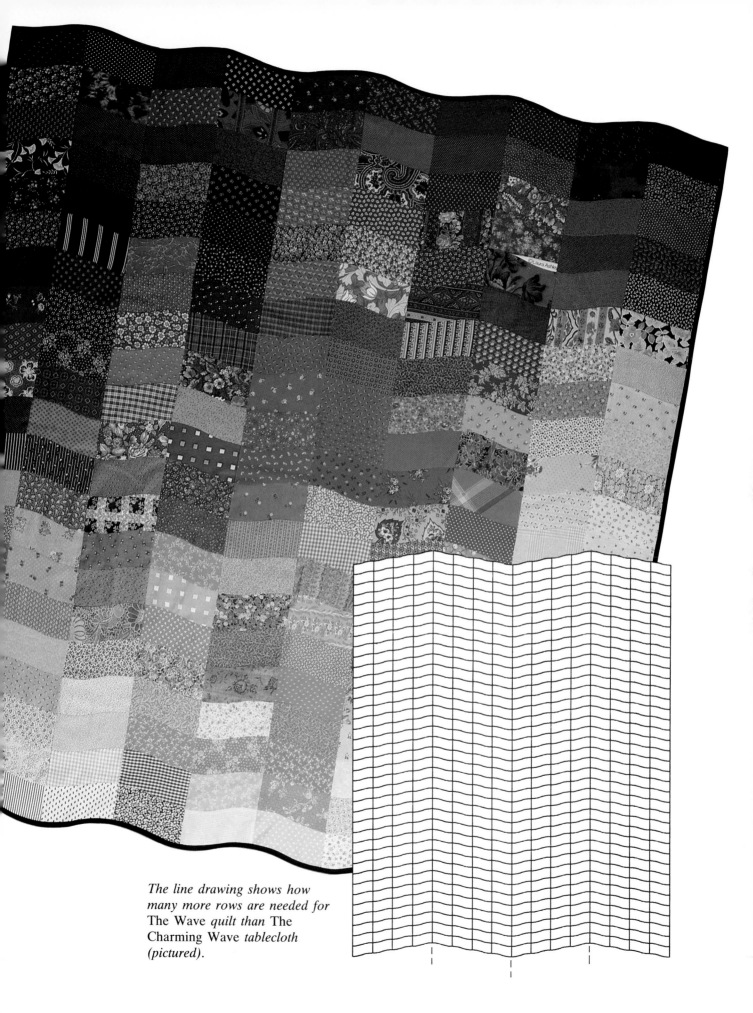

The line drawing shows how many more rows are needed for The Wave *quilt than* The Charming Wave *tablecloth (pictured).*

Freezer Paper Patchwork

I happened upon the possibilities for freezer paper when I began teaching my Year Quilt Class. As I showed students *Hey Diddle Diddle,* a cat design wall hanging that I began in class with teacher Pauline Burbidge, I bemoaned the fact that so many templates were needed. I knew that I would never finish it!

Then I overheard some students talking excitedly about freezer paper—how it's perfect for appliqué templates because the shiny side actually sticks to fabric when pressed with a warm iron. Well, I thought, if it's good for appliqué templates, why not patchwork templates? If I made the *Hey Diddle Diddle* templates from freezer paper, I could iron them directly to the fabrics, and the templates would remain attached to the fabric even during machine sewing. That would provide me with a stitching guide, something hand piecers have had that I have always envied.

Eager to experiment, I enlarged the cat design and traced it onto the dull side of freezer paper. (Since the image was not symmetrical, I traced the back of the design, so that the final image would not be reversed.) I decided to piece it vertically, so I drew vertical lines over the image every 1¼″ and voila! I had instant templates, which made it easy for me to finish my wall hanging.

INTERRUPTED RECTANGLE

The vertical lines in *Hey Diddle Diddle* divide the design into long thin rectangles. These rectangles are interrupted by the angled lines of the design. They delineate the individual templates to cut. *Midnight in the Mountains, Shadow Cats,* and *The Wild Goose* are also based on this technique.

In "Patterns & Designs" each of these designs is on a grid for enlarging. Enlarge the design directly onto the dull side of freezer paper (if asymmetrical, finished design will be reversed). Or create a full-size design and then transfer the back of the design to the dull side of freezer paper.

FREEZER PAPER PATCHWORK

Transfer back of design to dull
side of freezer paper.*

1. Coding Rows and Templates.
On freezer paper drawing, draw
vertical or horizontal rows. Code
design with indelible pen. Label
rows A, B, C, left to right or
center outward, depending on
where you begin attaching rows.
Number templates top to bottom. Indicate color and grain
line.

2. Cutting Fabric Strips. Using a
rotary cutter and see-through
ruler, cut strips of fabric ½″
wider and longer than your rows
or templates, for seam allowances. Cut several fabrics at once
to save time.

3. Cutting Freezer Paper Strips.
Cut the freezer paper design
apart in rows, using the rotary
cutter or paper scissors. (Be sure
to keep a copy of the original
design for reference when piecing your design.)

4. Cutting Templates. Cut one
row at a time into individual templates. Complete all remaining
steps for this row before continuing with the next row. (These
templates can be saved and used
again.)

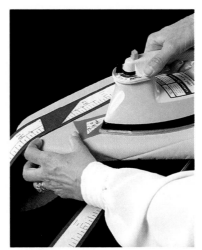

**5. Ironing Templates onto Fab-
ric.** With the shiny side down,
center the template on the wrong
side of the fabric strip and press.

6. Trimming Seam Allowances.
Use the rotary cutter and a see-
through ruler with a ¼″ marking
to trim your seam allowances to
¼″, or use scissors to trim seam
allowances that you have marked
first with chalk, making this a
two-step process.

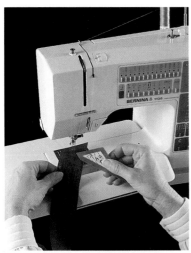

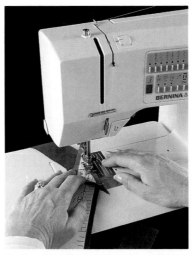

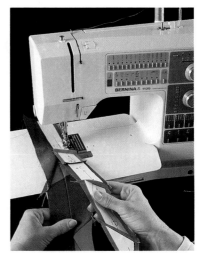

7. Aligning Templates. Hold adjoining fabric pieces up toward a light source, with right sides together, and align the edges of the templates.

8. Sewing Pieces Together. Using a normal stitch and matching thread, sew the pieces together. Check both sides to be sure the paper is not caught. If it is, rip out the seam and realign to sew again. Use pins to anchor longer seams together.

9. Sewing Rows Together. With right sides together and seams down, sew rows together. Use the templates as a stitching guide. Check to see that you don't catch the paper in your seam. *For information on gridded freezer paper, contact Lap Quilting, P.O. Box 96, Flat Rock, NC 28731.

Shadow Cats

Meow! Meow! Meow! The inspiration for this wall hanging was a piece of fabric with three little cats. Notice how the tails overlap and the forward kitty is a stronger color than the ones farther away. A 1"-square grid was used here, but as in any grid design, the size can be varied to suit each quilter.

Shadow Cats
Finished Size: 18" x 20"
Perimeter: 76"
Strip Piecing: 1" grid, 20 vertical rows and 18
    horizontal rows
Fabric Requirements:
   Cats: ½ yard each of three colors
   Background: ½ yard

Three cats sit prettily on this pieced wall hanging.

The stars and moon at midnight add wonder to the flexicurve mountains below.

Midnight in the Mountains

Strip piecing creates the stars, the moon, and the mountains at midnight. I like to call these stars five-pointed stars with personality. The stars and crescent moon shine down on the Blue Ridge Mountains, made with a draftsmen's flexible curve. To keep the wall hanging lightweight, sew the flexed area to a tear-away material rather than to a foundation that must be left inside. Stabilize the mountain area by keeping the outside fabric on the crosswise or straight of the grain—not the bias.

Midnight in the Mountains

Finished Size: 29″ x 24″

Perimeter: 106″

Strip Piecing: 3″ x 12″, 6″ x 14″, and 2″ x 14″ bands for sky

Border: 3″-wide blue print border

Fabric Requirements:

 Strips for sky: 1 yard

 Mountains: Assorted scraps of blue and green fabric

 Tear-away material: 9″ x 24″

 Backing: ½ yard

INSIDE QUILTING

With inside quilting, stitches show only on the back.

1. Pinning the Center Row. After piecing the rows together, place the wrong side of the top down. Align the center inside vertical seam with the center of the batting and backing. Fold half of the top back to reveal the center seam allowance and pin in place.

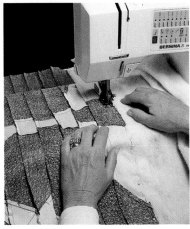

2. Quilting. Sew right on top of the previously sewn center seam, using a bobbin thread to match the backing.

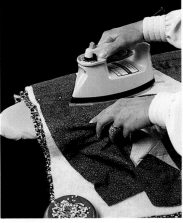

3. Pressing. Fold the panel forward and press the seam with a warm iron. To stabilize this row, pin every four to five inches.

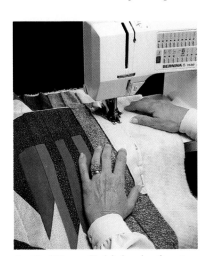

4. Quilting. Fold back the top again, revealing the next seam allowance. Quilt, stitching over the seam. Complete this half of the top; then complete the other side. Always begin stitching from the same direction.

This gander casts his shadow on the moon and flies into the night in a strip-picture piece.

The Wild Goose

The Wild Goose is the name of a quilt shop belonging to a friend of mine. Its banner is bound to catch the eyes of passersby. As with all strip-picture piecing, the templates in each row are determined by the angled lines created by the design (Figure A). The vertical strips in this design are 1½″ wide, but notice how some of the strips in the wing are divided in half to add more color and interest. Colorful bias fabric fringe completes the bottom.

The Wild Goose

Finished Size: 27″ x 36″ plus a 3″ fringe
Perimeter: 126″
Strip Piecing: 1½″ grid, 18 vertical rows and 24 horizontal rows
Fabric Requirements: Divide amount needed by the number of fabrics and colors used.
Background: 1 yard
Contrasting fabric: Small amount

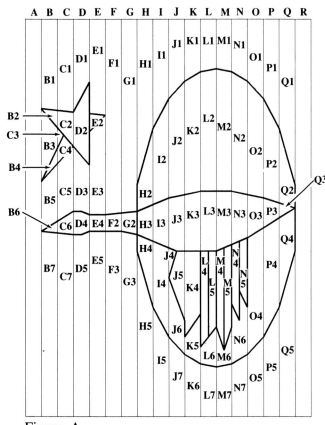

Figure A

Hey Diddle Diddle

The cat and the fiddle are busy playing on this colorful wall hanging. The curve of the cat's head, the fiddle, and garments all come together to form a flowing picture. To enlarge the design to the size shown (25″ x 32½″), draw a grid with 20 vertical rows and 26 horizontal rows, each 1¼″ apart. To complete the panel, follow the steps for freezer paper patchwork.

Cut the batting and backing 42″ x 53″ to allow for the borders, which are added later. Use inside quilting to quilt the panel. Then cut 3″-wide black sashing and sew around the panel.

To create the chevron border, sew the left-over colored fabric strips together into multicolored bands. Fold each band in half, wrong sides and short ends together and colors aligned. Cut a 45° angle at the folded end. From this cut, measure 3½″ and cut again. The cut pieces will be mirror images of one another. Alternating colors, sew all the same-shape pieces together to form one side of the chevron. Sew the mirror images together to form the other side. With wrong sides together and colors aligned, sew the sides together to form the chevron. Stitch small chevrons together to form the the top and bottom borders. Sew and flip the borders outward from the black sashing and press. Angles were left on the bottom for a banner effect.

Hand quilting is used to outline the figure, and the quilted musical notes in the border play "Hey Diddle Diddle," of course.

Hey Diddle Diddle

Finished Size: 42″ x 53″
Perimeter: 190″
Strip Piecing: 1¼″ grid, 20 vertical rows and 26 horizontal rows
Borders: 2½″-wide black sashing, 3½″-wide strips forming the chevron border
Fabric Requirements:
Colored fabrics: ½-yard lengths of six to ten fabrics
Background: 2 yards
Backing: 1½ yards

This gaily bedecked cat fiddles the tune of the nursery rhyme on a gray-tone backdrop.

68

PATCHWORK LETTERS

The idea of patchwork letters had always intrigued me, but I knew how many odd-shaped templates were required to form the letters—too many. Then came strip piecing with freezer paper.

The grid design given in "Patterns & Designs" is based on 1½" squares, so the rows of fabric are cut 2" wide. Notice that the nine asymmetrical letters in the grid are presented backwards. That means that as you enlarge the grid design and make the freezer paper templates you won't have to reverse these images. To border each letter, cut eight bias strips, 1⅝" wide and 9" long—four black and four to match the color of the letter. Sew these together, alternating colors. Next, cut across the rows every 1½", to form the angled border strips. Make the borders for each block and attach to all four sides.

Cut 3½" x 12½" sashing strips and attach between blocks as you sew the blocks into vertical rows. Cut three 3½" x 87½" sashing strips. Sew the sashing strips to the right of row B through V, C through W, and D through X. Once the rows are quilted and assembled, use the sew-and-extend method to attach the wide top and bottom borders with diagonal bands as accents. Quilt these borders; then attach the side borders, which include the letters A and Z, and quilt them.

The ABC Quilt

Finished Size: 81" x 111"
Perimeter: 384"
Blocks: Twenty-six 12" ABC blocks based on a
　1½" grid
Sashing: Twenty 3½" x 12½" strips and three
　3" x 87" strips
Borders:
　Top and bottom: 57½" x 11"
Sides: 87½" x 11"
Quilt: 1½"-wide yellow-and-black striped
　bias border
Fabric Requirements:
　Bright colors: 3 yards (divide by number of
　　fabrics used)
　Sashing, border, and background: 4 yards
　Backing: 6 yards

Watch your Ps and Qs and all those other bright letters, when piecing this alphabet.

Colorful sampler blocks represent my many cross-country flights to visit active quilters.

AN ASYMMETRICAL SAMPLER

It seems sampler quilts have been popular since quilting began. For most of us our first quilt was a sampler. In *More Lap Quilting,* I showed sophisticated samplers, sampler blocks arranged around a large center panel. Well, another arrangement for your blocks is in an asymmetrical sampler. Emphasize one block by enlarging it and then surround it with smaller blocks. That's exactly what I did in *Come Fly with Me.*

Come Fly with Me

This quilt is a tribute to the guilds, groups, and shops across America that further the study of quiltmaking. Each block in the quilt represents one of the many areas where I have taught and have been so warmly received.

The block An Aerial View is a study of

perspective within a 30″ square. To design this block, establish a point off the square; then using a yardstick, draw angled lines to that point. Add parallel horizontal lines to represent the lay of the land. After transferring this part of the design to freezer paper, code the horizontal rows and each template within the row. Follow the steps for freezer paper patchwork to complete the block. Use the flexible curve to create the purple mountains' majesty in the 10″ sky panel. Join the sky and the land before quilting. If you look carefully, you can see the shadow of the airplane created by the quilting.

Use the grid designs in "Patterns & Designs" and the freezer paper patchwork technique to create the Minnesota Loon, the New York Skyline, and the Canadian Maple Leaf. In the Minnesota Loon block, the bill of the loon reaches over into the 3″ border. This 12″ block is made up of fabric strips cut 2″ wide. The New York Skyline combines strips of different

body, etc., begin piecing by attaching the head to the body. Sew an arm to a pie shape and then attach to head and body. Attach the opposite arm and pie shape in the same manner. Sew the bottom left leg to a pie shape and attach to the arm and body. Sew the remaining leg between two pie shapes and attach to complete the circle. The remainder of the square can be aligned by matching side seams with template marks. Quilting lines depict the state of Texas with all roads leading to Houston, a focal point for yearly quilt meetings and markets.

N.E.H.C. stands for the National Extension Homemakers Council, adult continuing education through the land-grant colleges and agricultural extension services. This block celebrates the organization's 50th anniversary in Virginia. The ½″ letters are appliquéd on an appropriate background—a home.

Our national bird, the eagle, commemorates my travels out west. Here the eagle is in a 12″ block, but you will see it again in *Blue Ridge Beauty* as the central motif in a 20″ block.

The blocks in *Come Fly with Me* have endless possibilities. I have bordered each design with the Wings block because so many of my travels have been by air, and the land seen from the air is echoed in the parallelogram border.

widths, and the Canadian Maple Leaf has eight rows, each 1½″ wide.

The E.G.A. block recognizes the Embroidery Guilds of America, particularly the Dogwood chapter. The needle and thimble symbolize the guilds' concentration on fine needlework of all kinds. Use ½″ and ¼″ bias strips to appliqué the letters.

For the remaining blocks, templates are offered with the conventional ¼″ seam allowance. But if you decide to make the templates out of freezer paper, trace the broken line, not the solid line, onto the freezer paper. Then cut out the template and press it onto the fabric. Add a ¼″ seam allowance when cutting out the fabric.

The Pelican block represents Florida and all its sunshine. The bird is set on a field of blue and topped with a sailor's cap.

The corner block is for Texas—a five-pointed Texas star. If you picture the five-pointed star as a person (Figure B) with head,

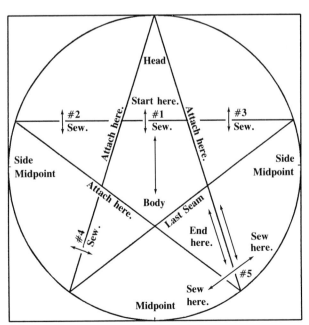

Figure B

Come Fly with Me

Finished Size: 78″ x 96″

Perimeter: 348″

Large block: 1. An Aerial View—30″ square (grid provided)

Sampler blocks: Eight 12″-square blocks
 2. Minnesota Loon (grid)
 3. New York Skyline (grid)
 4. Canadian Maple Leaf (grid)
 5. E.G.A., Embroidery Guild of America
 6. The Pelican
 7. Texas Star
 8. N.E.H.C., National Extension Homemakers Council
 9. The Eagle

Borders: Seventy-two 6″ Wings blocks, 3″-wide mitered borders for each block

Fabric Requirements:
 Blocks: ¼-yard pieces of assorted fabrics
 Mitered borders: 2½ yards
 Wings block: 1½ yards each of two colors

QUILTING FOR THE RED, WHITE & BLUE

Old Glory waving in the breeze, our national anthem sung at a ball game, the restoration of the Statue of Liberty, the birthday celebration of our Constitution—all are events to inspire the making of a patriotic quilt. It may be for a contest or to decorate your family room wall, but it seems that red, white, and blue reign when we celebrate our American spirit!

My Star-Spangled Banner

An American quilt, with five historic pieced symbols placed amidst a star background, exudes patriotism. The stars are created from a familiar block, the Log Cabin. This time, just two colors are used for the rectangles, radiating outward from the 1½″ center square. Even the solid red blocks are totally "log-cabined" to continue the piecing effect. The center square and strips are cut 1½″ wide. The 18″ squares could be adapted to any freezer paper sketch or other block design. Each design is set up on a grid with some horizontal and some vertical piecing. This quilt by Glennda Gussman, a member of the Year Quilt Class, is truly a proud accomplishment with a flag-waving theme.

My Star-Spangled Banner
Finished Size: 72″ x 72″
Perimeter: 288″
Log Cabin blocks: Forty-four 9″ blocks—twelve red blocks, thirty-two red-and-blue blocks
Strip-pieced blocks: Five 18″ blocks based on 1″-square grids
1. The Eagle
2. The Liberty Bell
3. The Conestoga Wagon
4. Stars and Stripes
5. The Statue of Liberty Torch
Fabric Requirements:
    Red: 1¾ yards
    Blue print: 1¾ yards
    Backing: 4½ yards

Log Cabin blocks aglow in red, white, and blue surround symbols of America.

Seeing Stars

This quilt was created under the guidelines of The Great American Quilt Contest and celebrates the renovation of the Statue of Liberty. My initial inspiration for it was the paisley border print fabric suggesting patriotism, but this design would be successful in many other color schemes. Rather than focus on the entire statue, I wanted to highlight the crown, so I repeated the design to form a large five-pointed star.

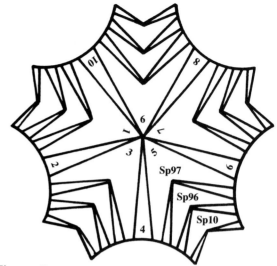

Figure C

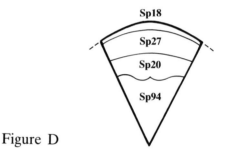

Figure D

Miss Liberty's crown radiates into a star.

Place background templates—Sp97, Sp96, and Sp10—on the fold of the fabric when cutting out. This helps eliminate some of the extra bulk at the center. Cut templates for the red points out of freezer paper. The freezer paper provides a sewing guide, which is especially important at the center point of the star. Trace the templates on the broken lines. Add your ¼″ seam allowance when you cut out the fabric. Piece the center crown area in a circular fashion following the number sequence given (Figure C). Then continue adding the shorter points and the background in each of the five crown areas.

Piece the head unit—Sp94, Sp18, and Sp27. Appliqué the hair, Sp20, in place (Figure D). Repeat for the other four head units. Then sew the head units to the center crown area.

For the border, points, and background—Sp48, Sp13, Sp84, Sp33, Sp95, and Sp31 are pieced as one continuous unit for each side. For the head unit, piece Sp28 and Sp17. Then appliqué Sp51 in place. Attach the head units to the crown area of the border. Miter the corners of the border at a 45° angle. Five large five-pointed stars are quilted in a circular pattern within the center circle, extending into the paisley border print. Two smaller stars, quilted in the blue area within each of the larger quilted stars, represent Lady Liberty's eyes.

Seeing Stars
Finished Size: 72″ x 72″
Perimeter: 288″
Border: Continuous 8″-wide crown border
Fabric Requirements: Divide amount by the number and colors of fabrics used.
  Front: 5 yards
  Backing: 4 yards

Sp84
Sp62
Sp33
Sp31
Sp95
Sp48
Sp13
Sp64

56˝

23¾˝ radius

11¾˝

28˝

12¾˝

Sp17
Sp28
Sp16
Sp51

The Fine Points of Quiltmaking

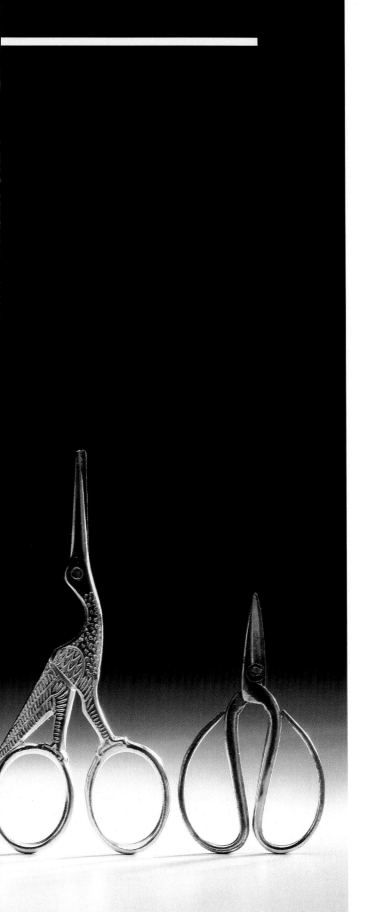

Has a trip to the annual quilt show left you haunted by the quilt with all the fine points? You've made that first sampler, and you're ready to tackle something new—but all those points! Don't let them intimidate you.

Here are a few suggestions to consider when making this type of quilt. When selecting color, create a contrast between the points and the diamonds. If you are using fabric with a large print, take advantage of the design by placing it in the identical position within the template each time you cut it out.

When piecing, use quick-piecing techniques or shortcuts. When possible, use a master template (a template equal in size to the assembled finished pieces) to check your progress before completing the sections. Press closed seams toward the darker fabric and eliminate as many dog ears as possible.

For quilts with a concentration of piecework such as these, elaborate quilting is easier if restricted to large unpieced areas. Around the fine points, outline quilting, or quilting close to the seam, is best so that quilting over seams can be avoided.

ELIMINATING BULKY INTERSECTIONS

Where seams join at right angles and at star intersections, there is always an excessive amount of bulk created by the seam allowances. This can cause the front of the block to be raised on one side of the seam. At last a solution! I picked up this technique in Billings, Montana, so I call it my Billings Bonus. I hope you'll find this hint helpful when stitching the quilts in this chapter.

79

ELIMINATING BULKY INTERSECTIONS

1. Sewing. Sew the intersection with closed staggered seams (raw edges of seam allowances going in different directions).

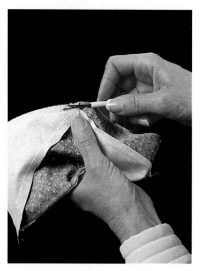

2. Ripping. With a pin or seam ripper, rip out only the stitches in the intersecting seam allowances.

3. Positioning Seams. Position the seams in a concentric circle.

Patchwork Jungle

As the number of pieces per block multiplies, so does the amount of patience and time needed to assemble the *Patchwork Jungle* wall hanging, but it's all worth the effort when completed. The Pine Burr block is a jewel of a design when combined with exotic prints. When piecing this block, concentrate on the smallest sections first. Use the master rectangle R14 to check the piecework. Follow the seven steps for piecing the sections of one Pine Burr block (Figure A). Multiply each step by number of blocks desired.

Patchwork Jungle
Finished Size: 39″ x 39″
Perimeter: 156″
Blocks: Four 18″ Pine Burr blocks
Borders: 1½″-wide pieced border
Fabric Requirements:
  Tropical print: 1½ yards
  Companion fabric: ½ yard each of 2 colors
  Backing: 1½ yards

The very fine points of an old favorite block take on a new look with a tropical print, culminating in Patchwork Jungle *by Shirley Klennon.*

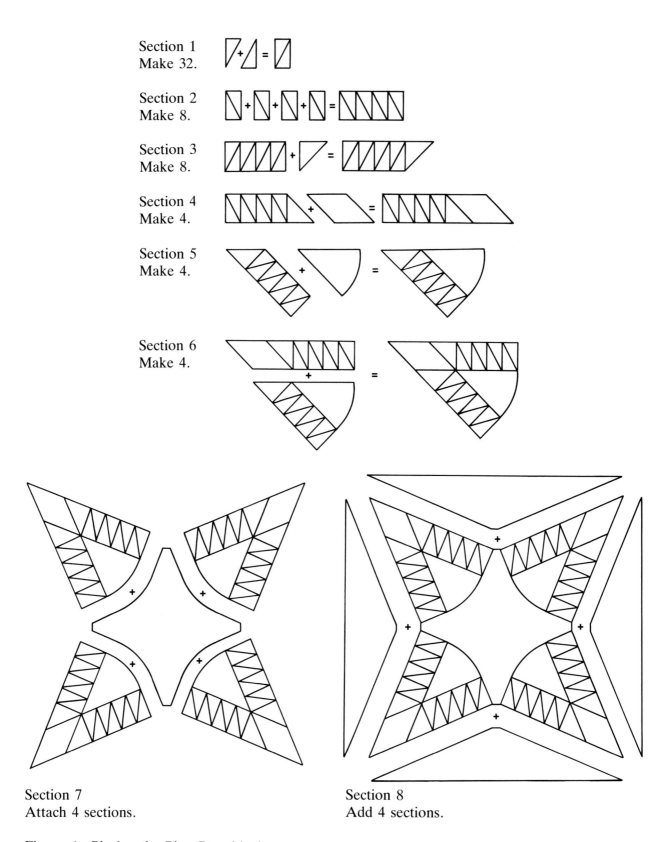

Section 1
Make 32.

Section 2
Make 8.

Section 3
Make 8.

Section 4
Make 4.

Section 5
Make 4.

Section 6
Make 4.

Section 7
Attach 4 sections.

Section 8
Add 4 sections.

Figure A: Piecing the Pine Burr block.

When the decisions of color and fabric selection are overwhelming, turn to—Just Muslin.

Just Muslin

Is fabric selection a dilemma for you? One way to solve the problem is to use a single fabric—just muslin. It simplifies things, but all of a sudden the seam allowances become an important design element. When the seam allowances are pressed, their outline can be seen on the surface of the block.

In this wall hanging, borders radiate from the center LeMoyne Star block. The first pieced border is made up of small triangles (T60) and squares (S4). The second pieced border uses larger triangles (T21) and 3″ squares (S13) in the corners. For the third border, ½″-wide bands are added to each side of the Flying Geese border (T21 and T60), making it the same width as the squares (S1) in the corners. To complete the wall hanging, a 1″-wide border and a 1½″-wide border are added.

Just Muslin
Finished Size: 34″ x 34″
Perimeter: 136″
Blocks: One 12″ LeMoyne Star block

Borders: Three pieced bands and two unpieced bands
Fabric Requirements:
  Muslin: 1½ yards
  Backing: 1 yard

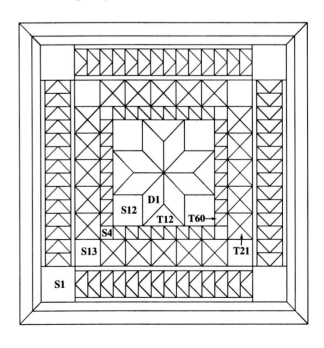

Feathered Star blocks blossom in print and points in Flowers That Bloom in the Spring.

Flowers That Bloom in the Spring

One of the most admired quilt patterns of all time, the Feathered Star, is a true accomplishment. The amount of quilting that Grace Anderson stitched in her Feathered Star quilt makes it extraspecial. The Feathered Star block bears a faint similarity to the Pine Burr block, but the triangles in Feathered Star form squares, rather than rectangles, when two are joined together. There are many ways to approach the piecing of this block, but after much testing, I feel this is the best way (Figure B).

Notice how the triangle and trapezoid spill out into the dark border. When using print fabric, if you place the template in exactly the same position on the design each time you cut it out, a unique repeat pattern is formed.

Flowers That Bloom in the Spring
Finished Size: 90¾" x 70¾"
Perimeter: 323"
Blocks: Twelve 20" Feathered Star blocks
Borders: 5⅞"-wide pieced border
Fabric Requirements:
  Blocks: 5½ yards of at least 3 or 4 fabrics
    (divide by number of fabrics used)
  Borders: 1½ yards
  Backing: 5 yards

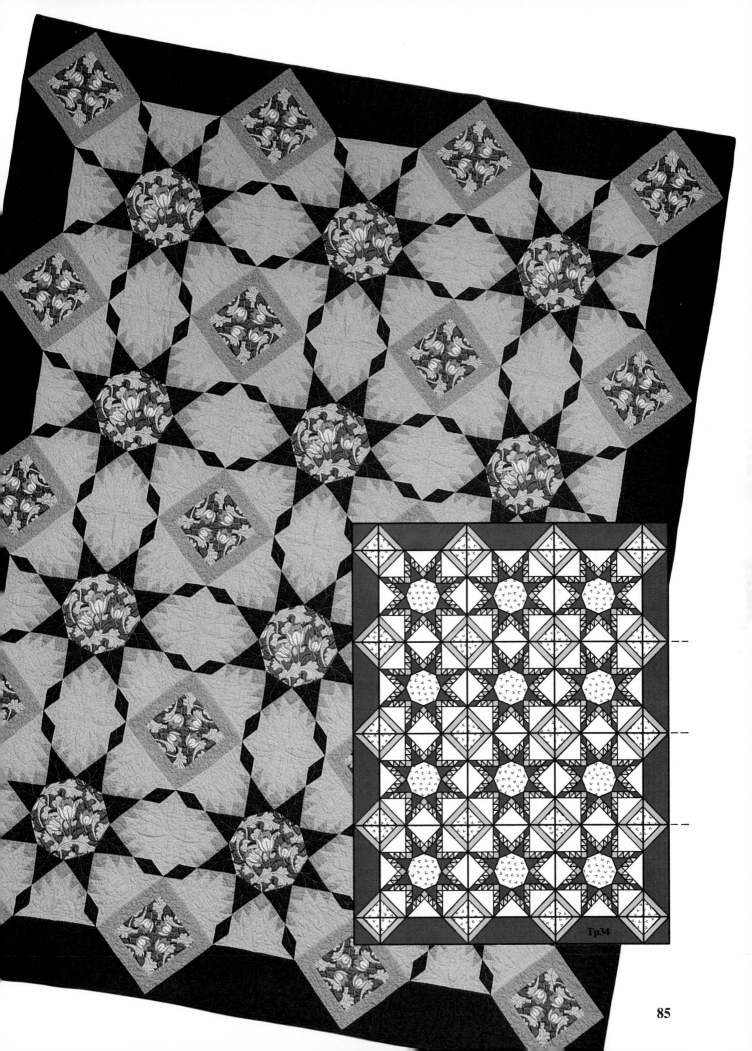

Tp34

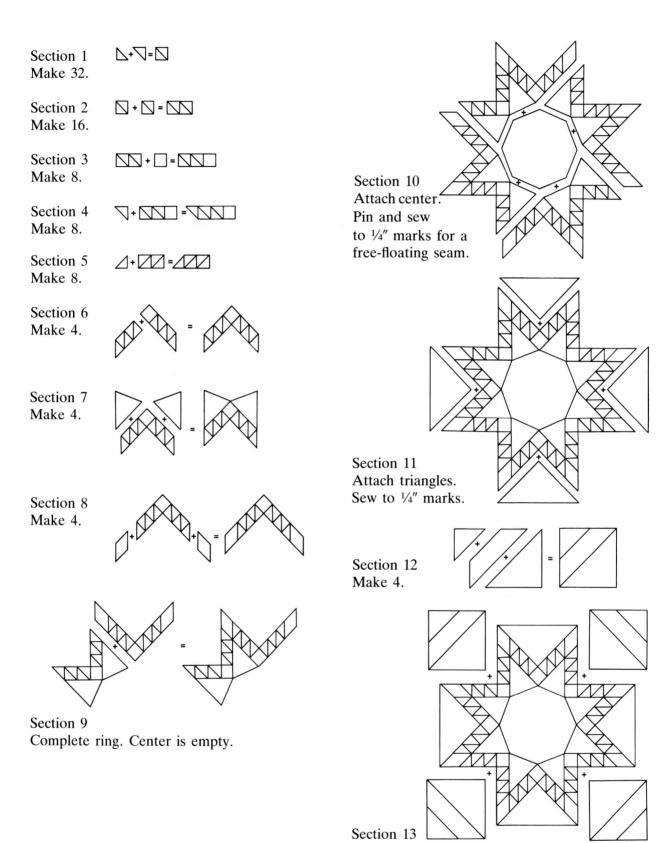

Section 1
Make 32.

Section 2
Make 16.

Section 3
Make 8.

Section 4
Make 8.

Section 5
Make 8.

Section 6
Make 4.

Section 7
Make 4.

Section 8
Make 4.

Section 9
Complete ring. Center is empty.

Section 10
Attach center.
Pin and sew
to ¼″ marks for a
free-floating seam.

Section 11
Attach triangles.
Sew to ¼″ marks.

Section 12
Make 4.

Section 13
Attach corners to complete block. Sew to ¼″
mark.

Figure B: Piecing the Feathered Star block.

TURNING TRIANGLES INTO SQUARES

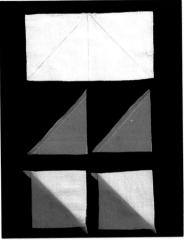

1. Tracing the Template. Place the right sides of two square pieces of contrasting fabric together. Align the grain line of a right angle triangle template with that of the fabric. This template includes the seam allowances. Trace around all three sides. Flip the template and trace again until you have four triangles.

2. Adding a Stitching Line and Sewing. Mark a broken line (stitching line) ¼″ on each side of each diagonal line or use the guide of the presser foot to establish a seam allowance. Stitch the two fabrics together.

3. Cutting the Fabric. Cut the fabric on the solid lines to reveal eight squares made up of contrasting triangles. Use the corner square in the block as a master template. It should be the same size as the squares made up of two triangles.

TURNING TRIANGLES INTO SQUARES

What looks like a very complicated triangular design can sometimes be done quickly and easily using this quick-piecing technique.

Odd Fellows Chain

One block design and four templates come together to form a dynamite black-and-white wall hanging. The distinct positive and negative contrast forms a crisp, sharp look. The corner triangles that create small squares can be quick-pieced by tracing template T60 72 times. Then check the size of the pieced squares with square template S4. The corner four-patches should be the same size as S13.

Triangles and squares create a dramatic, black-and-white Odd Fellows Chain.

Odd Fellows Chain

Finished Size: 48″ x 48″
Perimeter: 192″
Blocks: Nine 12″ blocks
Borders: Double 3″-wide borders
Fabric Requirements:
  Blocks: 1½ yards of two contrasting colors
  Borders: 1½ yards of two contrasting colors
  Backing: 2½ yards

The Maple Leaf Quilt

Group quilts are special, with many hands joining together for one cause. The cause this time was the Yadkin County Chapter of the American Heart Association. The 18 blocks set on point are made in a unique way. Each 6½″ square is trimmed with a narrow ½″-wide border before being joined to the others.

The triangle points of each maple leaf can be assembled easily and quickly with the quick-piecing method. Use the corner square in the Maple Leaf block as a master template. The squares made up of the two triangles should be the same size as the corner square.

These blocks, set on point, are framed by

triangles. The measurement for the triangles is given in the quilt diagram. Remember to add a ¼″ seam allowance on all sides when making the template. If you make the template from freezer paper, press the template onto the back of the fabric and cut ¼″ beyond the template for seam allowances. To increase the size of the quilt add a Delectable Mountain border. The overlapping heart quilting pattern is a fitting design for the American Heart Association.

The Maple Leaf Quilt

Finished Size: 81″ x 97″
Perimeter: 560″
Blocks: Eighteen 13½″ blocks
Borders: 9″-wide Delectable Mountain border, 2″-wide outside border
Fabric Requirements:
  Leaves: 2 yards of remnants
  Muslin: 4½ yards
  Backing: 6 yards

Fall colors come alive in an array of calico.

Kids' Play

P erpetuating our quilting heritage is important to all quilters. One way to do this is to teach quilting to young people. In planning the Kids' Play class, my goal was to introduce the basics of hand and machine sewing through the short, straight seams of patchwork. We decided to meet a couple of times each month for as long as it took to complete a small quilt. It took many months, as it turned out, because quilting had to take place between everyone's school schedule and outside activities. The first few lessons were spent threading a needle, learning the foolproof knot, and hand-sewing a small block. With each session we came closer to introducing the quilt pattern Stretched Stars. Once the pattern was explained and the steps for its completion outlined, I dangled a carrot in front of the class—to show off their quilts on television. This was an incentive to finish the projects.

STRETCHED STARS

The design for our class was made up of 3″ squares with triangles sewn in opposite corners. When the squares are sewn together they form the stars. The design can grow and grow or stop at pillow size. The stars can even be placed at random, not covering every square.

The base foundations used by the class varied. Some students used muslin; others used pretty peach and blue fabrics. Since the girls had drawn the full-size design on paper, they had a place to pin the squares and watch the design grow as they sewed. Because the triangles were sewn and flipped onto the 3½″ square base, instead of pieced, we didn't have two raw edges to align. So we had to improvise with the students. In the corner of the square, we positioned the small triangle template (Figure A) so that we could trace the diagonal edge. Then we aligned the diagonal edge of the fabric triangle (right side down and right angle toward square's center) with the traced line. The triangle was then sewn and flipped into position. Right angles of the triangle and square had to match, or we ripped out and tried again.

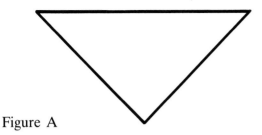

Figure A

Stretched Stars
Finished Size: 27″ x 21″
Perimeter: 96″
Borders: Optional
Fabric Requirements:
    Foundation: 1½ yards muslin or other fabric
        of your choice
    Stars: Small amount of scraps

Triangles turned squares into Stretched Stars, *as many fingers stitched their first quilts.*

A LESSON PLAN

To teach this pattern to children, I would suggest scheduling ten classes, or more if necessary, so students can finish their projects. Schedule about 1½ hours for each class. This seems about the right amount of time, not too long, but long enough to accomplish something.

Kids' Play Class—Front row: Elizabeth Phipps, Elizabeth Wilson. Back row: Betsy Freeman, instructor, Allison Kissling; Sherry Ball, instructor, Anna Weber, Kristin Hadley, Rachel Ferguson, Georgia Bonesteel, instructor. Not pictured: Emery Boyd.

Gathered around the table, the girls learn the next step in quiltmaking.

Elizabeth learned her lessons well and completed her little quilt.

Week One
Explain sewing terms and show examples.
    fabric
    patterns for garments
    needles
    templates for quilting
    thread
    grain line (crosswise and straight of grain)
    scissors
    bias

Week Two
Thread needle and demonstrate a foolproof knot. Have students practice this until they feel accomplished. Sew a four-patch block together in class, using a ¼″ seam allowance. Demonstrate how to add a border.

Week Three
Show off the students' handwork from last week. Be sure to praise work well done. Introduce several different models of sewing machines. Name the parts of the machine. Demonstrate threading both the top and the bobbin and have the students practice threading all the models. For practice at the machine have students sew on paper, following specified lines. It is easy to check the stitches on paper.

Week Four
Introduce the master plan for the small quilt. Have students draw a full-scale model on paper and color the triangles to form the stars.

Week Five
Cut out the pattern pieces. Cut 3½″ squares from fabric and pin to the drawings. For each star, cut out all six triangles from one fabric. Pin the triangles in place to form the star.

Week Six
Start sewing. Position the small triangle (Figure A) in opposite corners of the cloth squares and trace the diagonal edge with a pencil. Align the raw edge of the fabric triangle (right sides together) with the pencil line. Stitch ¼″ in from the raw edge and flip back.

Anna contemplates her quilting lines.

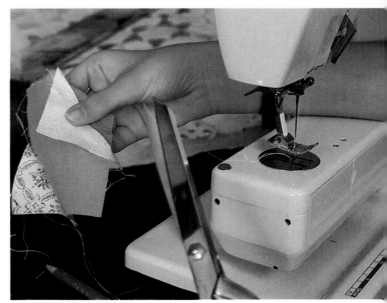

Little hands and big scissors trim the dog ears after sewing the triangles.

Week Seven
Continue sewing. Check students' piecing to make sure the triangles align with the 90° angle of each square's corner. If triangles don't align, rip them out. Check the piecing with master template S13.

Week Eight
Begin sewing rows. Once squares are completed, sew them together to form rows and then sew the rows together to complete the top. Stress ironing between piecing steps.

Week Nine
Cut out batting and backing. Align the top with the batting and backing. Pin all four corners and baste the layers together. Mark quilting lines (encourage straight lines) with a water-soluble marking pen.

Week Ten
Begin quilting. (It may be easier for some students to use a hoop.) Once quilting is completed, have students apply bias binding. Demonstrate how to make a bias tube.

DO'S AND DON'TS FOR TEACHING KIDS

Kids can quilt, but there are some special things to consider. Before approaching a class you might want to review these do's and don'ts.

Do have short sessions—no longer than 1½ hours each.
Do explain the basic tools of the trade: thread, needles, scissors, templates, etc.
Do show hand sewing first.
Do have an enthusiastic helper.
Do be patient.
Do be flexible.
Do serve some snacks or cold drinks.
Do encourage the students to show their parents what they have learned at each session.
Don't be too demanding.
Don't lose your sense of humor.
Don't forget to elevate their seats at the sewing machines.
Don't expect perfect attendance.
Don't expect perfect work.
Don't forget to have fun.

In this day and age we are all tuned in to quick quilting. "Make it today; sleep under it tomorrow" seems to echo our natural penchant for speed and accomplishment. But have you thought about putting on the brakes and making a quilt over the period of a year? That's exactly what we did in our Year Quilt Class. We wanted to slow down in order to appreciate the steps in quiltmaking—one phase at a time.

This particular class was conducted through the understanding auspices of the Blue Ridge Technical College in Hendersonville, North Carolina. We had four six-week sessions, which happened to correspond with the seasons of the year. With each new session a new topic was emphasized: design, color, piecing, and quilting. The objectives of the sessions varied, but students could enter the beginning class of any session if they had met the requirements of the previous one. To top off our year's study, we had a gallery exhibition of our quilts entitled, "A Show of Hands."

DESIGN

The first session occurred in the springtime, a time for budding new ideas. We concentrated on design by studying past and present quilts, hoping to gain an understanding of balance and perspective. To better use the drafting tools available to us, we invited a guest draftsman to speak to the class. Practice exercises helped us comprehend more difficult designs and enabled us to mix them with traditional patterns.

In designing, we considered the bed size, along with templates and block settings. The quilts the students designed to work on for the entire year included patriotic quilts, picture quilts, and even future prize-winning quilts. We learned that we needed to be flexible and willing to alter original ideas. Sometimes we found it helpful to obtain outside advice. As we prepared a small graph of the overall design and colored in areas, we began to dream of and ponder the next class—color and fabric.

The Haunted Mill of Willow Creek

Mary Berry's quilt exemplifies the work accomplished in our design class. The inspiration for her quilt was an old mill near her home. To help design her block, she brought photographs of the mill to class. She used rectangles to form the door and window area of the angled house. The parallelograms used for the diagonal roofs were attached with a free-floating mitered seam. (Sew up to the ¼" mark to create the free-floating seams.) Then the background sky templates were attached to the side and roof. Mary sewed the waterwheel wedges together and added the curved piece. To complete and enlarge the block, triangles (T48 grainline #2) were sewn to all four sides. Part of the wheel extends into those triangles.

Once Mary finished the mill block, we were stumped as to a suitable setting. The angles of her block were reminiscent of Nancy Halpern's work, so a consultation letter to Nancy and her subsequent reply helped Mary to plan the quilt on paper. Mary decided to use 23 blocks, reversing eight of them. A zigzag border (cut on bias) was added to suggest the cascading stream. The waterwheel motif is repeated on the edge of the quilt between rows. The wedges are pieced first, the curves added, and then the wheel is set in twelve times.

The Haunted Mill of Willow Creek

Finished Size: 105" x 131"
Perimeter: 472"
Blocks: Twenty-three 12" blocks
Borders: 4"-wide sashing, twelve waterwheels
Fabric Requirements:
  Blocks: 4 yards (divide by number and color of fabrics used)
  Border and sashing: 3 yards
  Backing: 7 yards

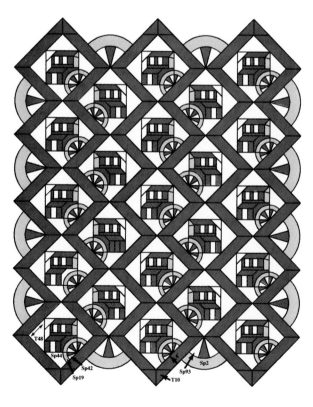

Not your "run of the mill" quilt, The Haunted Mill of Willow Creek *is a study of the mill from dusk till dawn.*

Starlit Flower Garden

Mary Ruth Branyon's garden quilt grew out of a special floral fabric. The print became the center of the nine-patch block, Fifty-four Forty or Fight. Alternating that block with a variation of Star Daze in a block-to-block quilt setting created a blue Orange Peel design.

This quilt is composed of two alternating nine-patch blocks. The four-patch squares and the diagonally pieced squares are perfect places to use quick-piecing techniques. Use a 4½″ square as a master template to check each patch.

Starlit Flower Garden

Finished Size: 76″ x 76″
Perimeter: 304″
Blocks: Twenty-five 12″ blocks—twelve Fifty-four Forty or Fight blocks, thirteen Star Daze blocks
Borders: Double 4″-wide borders
Fabric Requirements:
  Blocks and borders: 1 yard each of four colors
  Center squares of blocks: 1 yard of print
  Backing: 4½ yards

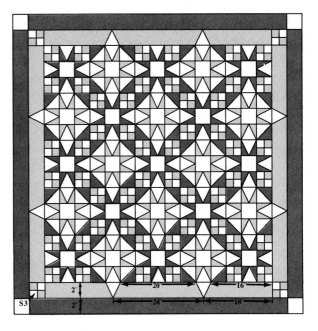

Squares and triangles form a striking blue secondary oval design in Starlit Flower Garden.

Pink and yellow stars radiate from a blue background in Starglow, *a shining example of color use.*

COLOR

Our goal for the summer session was to select the colors and fabrics for each quilt. We began with a study of the color wheel. To further explore fabric and color, we dyed and marbleized cloth. Both ventures were messy but productive, and lots of fun. Seeing that fabric in a finished quilt was especially gratifying. We also took field trips to an engraving plant and to a fabric-printing company. Search your community and you will probably find a factory that relates to quiltmaking and would be worth a visit.

Starglow

This quilt by Peggy Genung is a great example of how to use color successfully to enhance a design. Yellow is the focal point in this color arrangement. The lighter center radiates outward to a 4″-wide blue-gray border punctuated by pink triangles. The triangles are separated by rectangles (cut 4½″ x 8½″). A 2″-wide border completes the quilt.

Starglow
Finished Size: 96″ x 72″
Perimeter: 336″
Blocks: Thirty-five 12″ blocks—eighteen
    Starglow #1, seventeen Starglow #2
Borders: 4″-wide inside pieced border,
    2″-wide outside border
Fabric Requirements:
    Top: 7 yards (divide by number and
        color of fabrics used)
    Borders: 2 yards
    Backing: 6 yards

4" x 8"   4"   4"

6"

Sp63

Melody of the Blues

Marjorie Smith's quilt is made up of twenty enlarged Mexican Star blocks. As her quilt grew, her supply of blue calico dwindled, which meant introducing new shades of blue fabric and more blue print fabric. This certainly prevented the overly coordinated look that we sometimes regret. A medley of assorted blues sets off the border.

Melody of the Blues

Finished Size: 84″ x 100″
Perimeter: 368″
Blocks: Twenty 16″ Mexican Star blocks
Borders: 10″-wide pieced border with 2″-wide bands on both sides
Fabric Requirements:
  Top: 7 yards (divide by number and color of fabrics used)
  Backing: 6 yards

An enlarged Mexican Star design and many shades of blue create Melody of the Blues. *A border of rectangular bars amplifies the range of blues.*

Blue Ridge Beauty *is a patriotic tribute to the mountains of North Carolina.*

PIECEWORK

Finally in the fall, the production class began. I introduced piecing techniques that related to the many and varied quilts in the class. Students also brought their own piecing problems to class, and special dilemmas and decisions relating to seams, sequence of stitching, and border application were solved.

The constant feedback and the progress achieved each week kept us motivated. It was at this point in our class, however, that some students strayed. Moving, hospital stays, children coming and going, and quilt contest deadlines put some of us off-schedule.

Blue Ridge Beauty

Jan Zimmerman's many-faceted quilt builds from the center outward, containing new angles at every turn. The American Eagle block, seen in *Come Fly with Me*, is enlarged here to form a striking 20″ block. The eagle is surrounded by four 6″ Tulip Tree blocks and four 6″ Pine Tree blocks. The Delectable Mountain border provides a fitting finish for this tribute to the Blue Ridge Mountains.

Blue Ridge Beauty

Finished Size: 76½″ x 76½″

Perimeter: 288″

Blocks: One 20″ Eagle block, four 6″ Tulip Tree blocks, four 6″ Pine Tree blocks

Borders: 1½″-wide, 1″-wide, and ½″-wide borders surround eagle; 1″-wide, 1″-wide, and 2½″-wide borders surround center section; 1¼″-wide and 2½″-wide outside borders

Fabric Requirements:

Top: 7 yards (divide by number and color of fabrics used)

Backing: 5 yards

QUILTING

The final session occurred during the winter, an inviting time to spend indoors completing that all-important last phase—basting and quilting. We discussed our quilting options. Quilting lines could be compatible with their blocks—that is, lines that follow the lines of the piecework. Or quilting could be contrary and complement the piecing by creating a secondary line. Our means of quilting were as varied as we were. Some of us lap-quilted without frames, some quilted in hoops, and others quilted on a frame.

Ribbons of Blue

Two traditional blocks, Star Flower and Ribbon, come together in this nine-block setting by Ann DeBlois. A diamond motif is created by the large blue triangles in the Ribbon block. A corner trapezoid pulls the chevron border resembling twisted ribbons around each corner. Piecing the diamond shapes in the border requires carefully stitching up to the ¼″ seam.

Each triangular patchwork point is softened with arc and floral quilting lines. But, when necessary, straight lines on the blue calico add a special dimension.

Ribbons of Blue
Finished Size: 48″ x 48″
Perimeter: 192″
Blocks: Nine 12″ blocks—five Star Flower blocks; four Ribbon blocks
Borders: 4″-wide chevron border with four 5″ pieced corners; 1″-wide outer border
Fabric Requirements:
  Top: 4 yards (divide by number of fabrics used)
  Backing: 3 yards

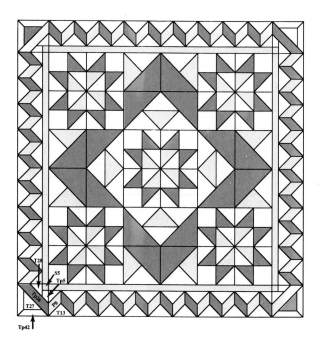

A twisted ribbon border surrounds the blue-and-rose stars in Ribbons of Blue.

The Year Quilt Class was made up of a dedicated group of quilters. Front row, left to right: Peggy Genung, Madge Townley, Mary Ruth Branyon. Second row, left to right: Mildred Ekback, Mary Berry, Sharon Phipps, Joan Pierro, Georgia Bonesteel, Ann DeBlois, Virginia Brower, Jean Novak, Lien Van Wagtendonk, Mary Bowen. Not pictured: Glennda Gussman, Marjorie Smith, Jan Zimmerman. Some of the quilts pictured are not presented in the book as patterns, since they are one-of-a-kind designs.

A LESSON PLAN

This class wasn't a contest, but a learning experience with one goal in mind—to finish an original quilt in a sharing atmosphere. If you can't find a class, gather some eager friends and use the following lesson plan to help you organize yourselves. Each quilt you complete will become filled with the stories of your experiences and memories shared with one another.

Session One

1. Draw simple four-patch and nine-patch block designs, with borders and without borders. Arrange in block-to-block settings.
2. Plan overall quilts for a particular bed size.
3. Arrange for a draftsman to visit and explain shapes and drafting terms.
4. Practice enlarging and reducing shapes.
5. Draft a star pattern.
6. Discuss grain line directions, template selection, and borders.
7. Develop a theme for a quilt contest or a logo.
8. Draw a scaled-down version of a proposed quilt and the full-size templates.
9. Present a slide show of both traditional and contemporary quilts.

Session Two

1. Report on a color and its closest tint and shade.
2. Create a color wheel from fabric.
3. Dye fabric (outdoor activity).
4. Marbleize fabric (outdoor activity).
5. Visit a factory related to cloth production.
6. Select fabrics and preshrink before next class.

Session Three

1. Trace templates onto fabric and cut out.
2. Demonstrate quick-piecing techniques.
3. Experiment with freezer paper templates.
4. Practice piecing inside right angles.

Session Four

1. Discuss and present the various types of batting and their particular characteristics.
2. Demonstrate contrary and compatible quilting lines.
3. Practice using tools to mark quilting lines.
4. Present demonstrations of a quilter using a standing frame and lap-quilting with and without a hoop. Discuss types of quilting thread.
5. Demonstrate how to lap-quilt a block-to-block connection and a row-to-row connection.
6. Review attaching borders and bindings.

Block designs, gridded designs, and geometric and appliqué templates for the quilts found throughout the book are included in this chapter. The block designs are arranged according to the challenge they might provide the quilter—Beginning, Intermediate, and Advanced. Though most of the block designs shown here are the same size, sizes of the actual blocks vary. Therefore the block size, along with the templates and the number of pieces, is listed with the block design. The shadings of the designs are merely suggestions and are there to help you distinguish the individual pieces.

Grids are given for the strip-piecing pictures. Specific instructions on how to enlarge a pattern are included in "Cotton Kivvers," and information on how to strip-piece is found in "Freezer Paper Patchwork."

The templates include the grain line and the ¼" seam allowances. They are grouped according to shapes.

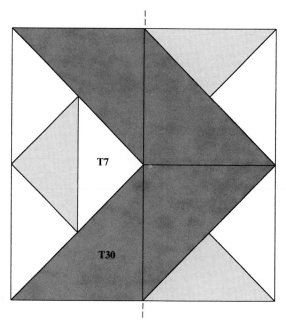

Ribbon
12" block
2 templates; 12 pieces
T7 (3 dk.; 5 lt.)   T30 (4)

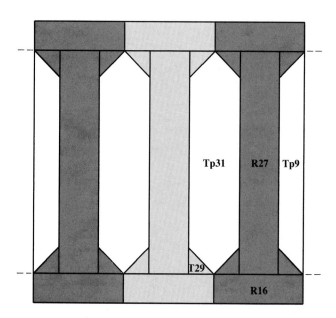

Wooden Thangs
12" block
5 templates; 25 pieces
T29 (12)   R27 (3)   Tp31 (2)
R16 (6)   Tp9 (2)

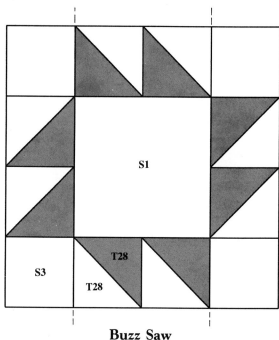

Buzz Saw
8" block
3 templates; 21 pieces
T28 (16)   S1 (1)   S3 (4)

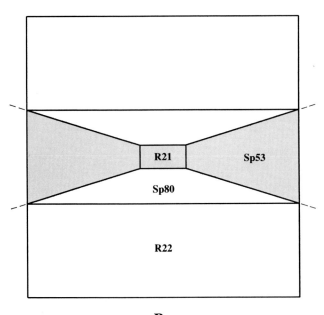

Bow
12″ block
4 templates; 7 pieces
R21 (1)   R22 (2)   Sp53 (2)   Sp80 (2)

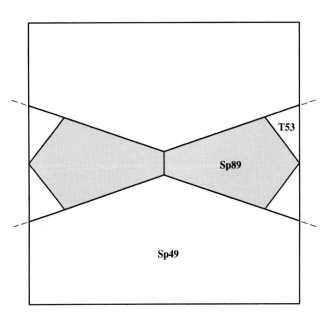

Tie
12″ block
3 templates; 8 pieces
T53 (4)   Sp49 (2)   Sp89 (2)

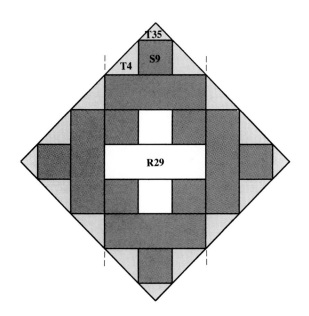

Album Block
8″ block
4 templates; 31 pieces
T4 (12 lt.) grainline #2   S9 (8 dk.; 2 lt.)
T35 (4 lt.)   R29 (4 dk.; 1 lt.)

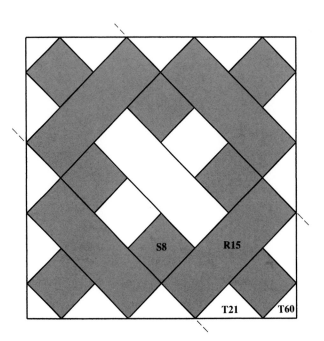

Freedom Escape—Album Block
12″ block
4 templates; 31 pieces
T21 (12)   R15 (4 dk.; 1 lt.)
T60 (4)   S8 (8 dk.; 2 lt.)

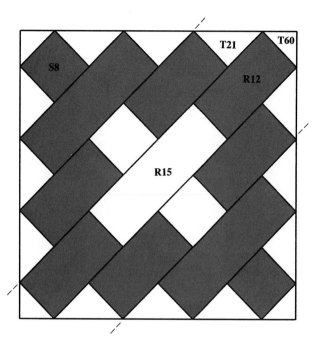

For Ellen—Album Block
12″ block
5 templates; 29 pieces
T21 (12)   R12 (6)   S8 (4)
T60 (4)   R15 (1 lt.; 2 dk.)

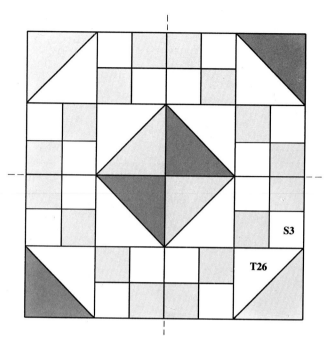

Jewelry Box
16″ block
2 templates; 48 pieces
T26 (16)   S3 (32)

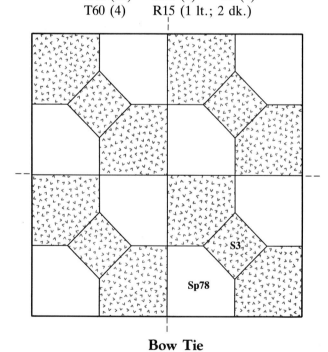

Bow Tie
12″ block
2 templates; 20 pieces
S3 (4 dk.)   Sp78 (8 lt.; 8 dk.)

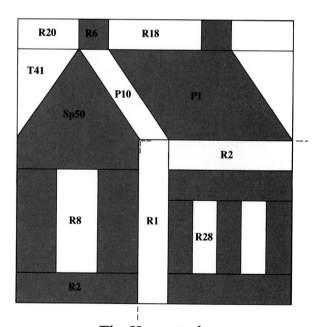

The Homestead
14″ block
11 templates; 23 pieces
T41 (2)   R6 (2)   R20 (2)   P10 (1)
R1 (1)   R8 (3)   R28 (5)   Sp50 (1)
R2 (4)   R18 (1)   P1 (1)

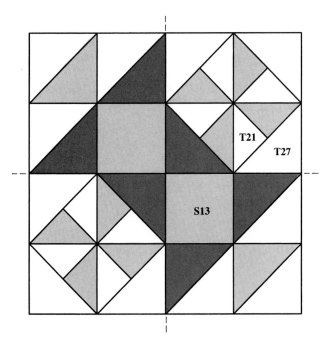

Hither and Yon
12″ block
3 templates; 38 pieces
T21 (16)   T27 (20)   S13 (2)

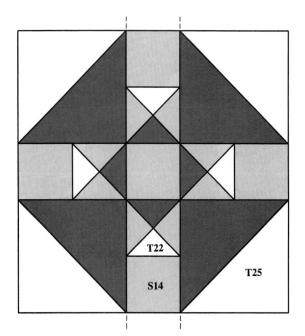

Mary Lee We Roll Along
12″ block
3 templates; 29 pieces
T22 (16) grainline #2   S14 (5)
T25 (8)

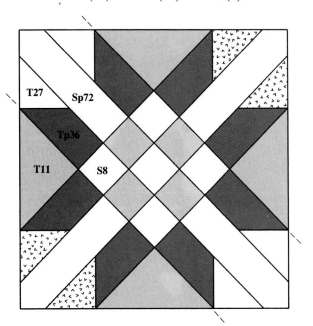

Mexican Star
16″ block
5 templates; 33 pieces
T11 (4)   Tp36 (8)   Sp72 (4)
T27 (8)   S8 (5 dk.; 4 lt.)

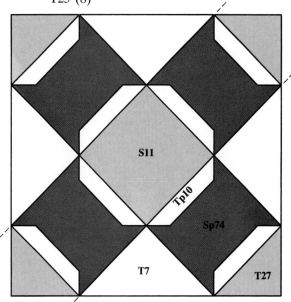

Secret Drawer
12″ block
5 templates; 21 pieces
T7 (4)   Tp10 (8)   Sp74 (4)
T27 (4)   S11 (1)

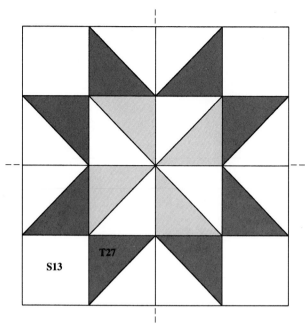

Star Flower
12″ block
2 templates; 28 pieces
T27 (12 dk.; 12 lt.)   S13 (4)

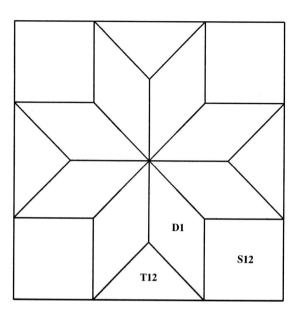

Just Muslin
12″ block
3 templates; 16 pieces
T12 (4)   S12 (4)   D1 (8)

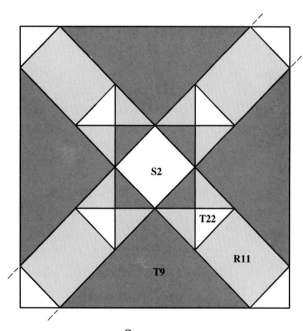

Spyrogyro
12″ block
4 templates; 29 pieces
T9 (4)   R11 (4)   S2 (1)
T22 (20) grainline #1

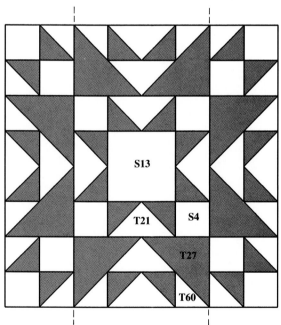

Odd Fellows Chain
12″ block
5 templates; 73 pieces
T21 (12)   T60 (40)   S13 (1)
T27 (8)   S4 (12)

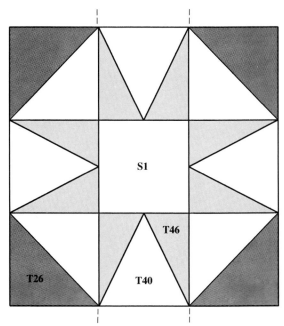

Star Daze Variation
12″ block
4 templates; 21 pieces
T26 (8)   T40 (4)   T46 (8)   S1 (1)

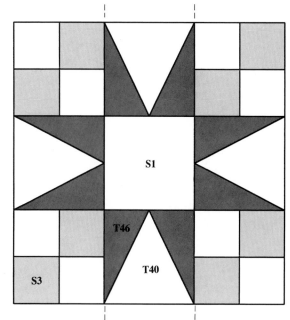

Fifty-four Forty or Fight
12″ block
4 templates; 29 pieces
T40 (4)   T46 (8)   S1 (1)   S3 (16)

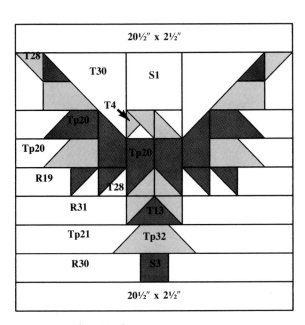

Blue Ridge Beauty—Eagle
20″ block
12 templates; 51 pieces
T4 (1 lt.; 1 bright) grainline #2
T28 (9 lt.; 8 dk.; 1 contrast; 1 bright)
T13 (1)   R30 (2)   Tp21 (2)   S1 (1lt.)
T30 (2 lt.)   R31 (2)   Tp32 (1)   S3 (1)
R19 (2)   Tp20 (6 lt.; 10 dk.)

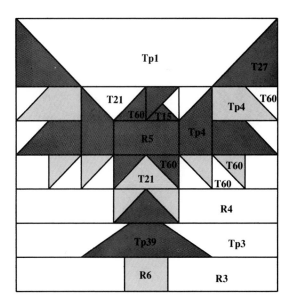

Come Fly with Me—Eagle
12″ block
13 templates; 44 pieces
T15 (2)   R3 (2)   Tp1 (1)   S3 (2)
T21 (3)   R4 (2)   Tp3 (2)
T27 (2)   R5 (1)   Tp4 (6)
T60 (19)   R6 (1)   Tp39 (1)

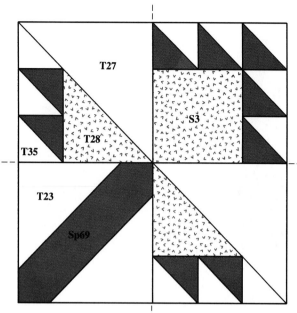

Tulip Tree
6″ block
6 templates; 28 pieces

T23 (2) T28 (2) S3 (1)
T27 (2 lt.) T35 (11 lt.; 9 dk.) Sp69 (1)

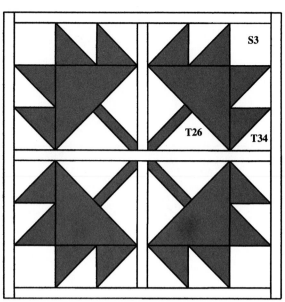

Maple Leaf
13½″ block
3 templates; 44 pieces (appliqué stems)
T26 (4 dk.; 4 lt.) S3 (4)
T34 (16 dk.; 16 lt.)

E.G.A.
12″ block—appliqué letters
A—½″ bias; E & G—¼″ bias
Form a needle and thimble for center;
flowers are optional.

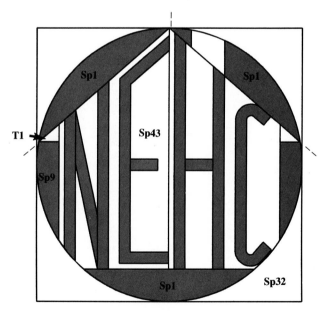

N.E.H.C.
12″ block
5 templates; 13 pieces
(appliqué letters N.E.H.C. and chimney)
T1 (2) Sp9 (2) Sp43 (2)
Sp1 (3) Sp32 (4)

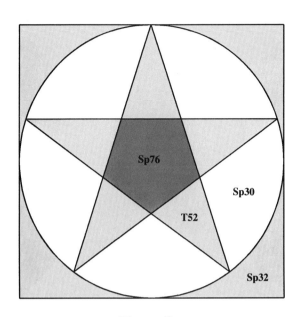

Texas Star
12″ block
4 templates; 15 pieces

T52 (5)   Sp30 (5)   Sp32 (4)   Sp76 (1)

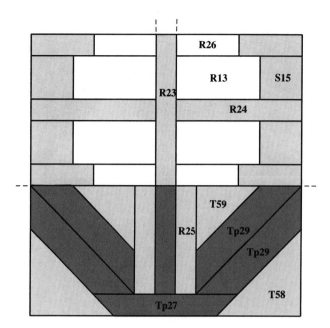

Pretty Posy
12″ block
10 templates; 31 pieces

T58 (2)	R23 (1)	R26 (8)	S15 (4)
T59 (2)	R24 (2)	Tp27 (1)	
R13 (4)	R25 (3)	Tp29 (4)	

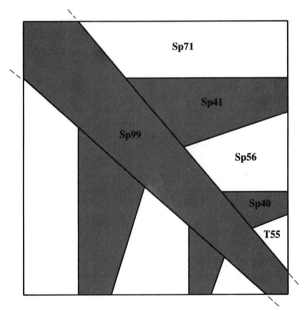

Wings
6″ block
6 templates; 11 pieces

T55 (2)	Sp41 (2)	Sp71 (2)
Sp40 (2)	Sp56 (2)	Sp99 (1)

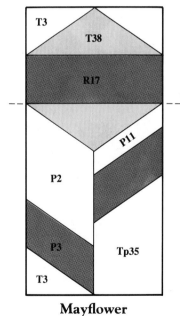

Mayflower
6″ x 12″ block
7 templates; 11 pieces

T3 (3)	R17 (1)	P2 (1)	P11 (1)
T38 (2)	Tp35 (1)	P3 (2)	

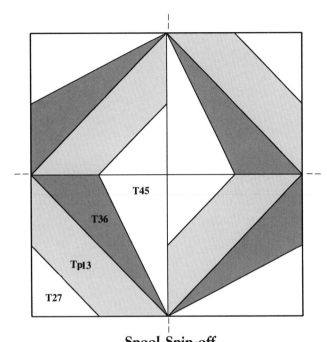

Spool Spin-off
12″ block
4 templates; 16 pieces
T27 (4)   T36 (4)   T45 (4)   Tp13 (4)

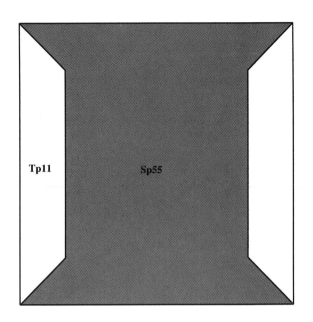

Spool Border Insert
3″ block
2 templates; 3 pieces
Tp11 (2)   Sp55 (1)

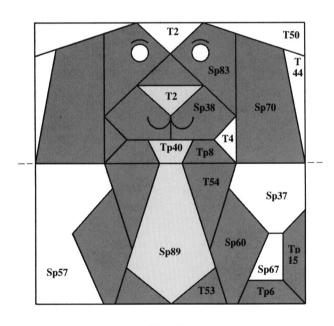

Tie Dog
12″ block
18 templates; 30 pieces

T2 (3)	T54 (2)	Tp40 (1)	Sp70 (2)
T44 (2)	Tp6 (1)	Sp37 (1)	Sp67 (1)
T50 (2)	Tp8 (2)	Sp38 (2)	Sp83 (2)
T53 (2)	Tp15 (1)	Sp57 (1)	Sp89 (1)
T4 (2) grainline #2		Sp60 (2)	

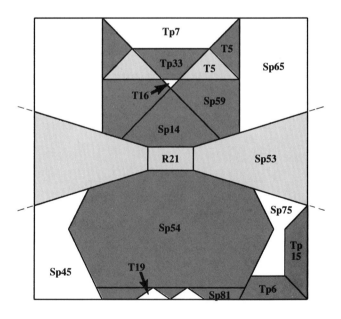

Bow Cat
12″ block
16 templates; 25 pieces

T5 (4)	Tp6 (1)	Sp14 (1)	Sp59 (2)
T16 (1)	Tp7 (1)	Sp45 (1)	Sp65 (2)
T19 (3)	Tp15 (1)	Sp53 (2)	Sp75 (1)
R21 (1)	Tp33 (1)	Sp54 (1)	Sp81 (2)

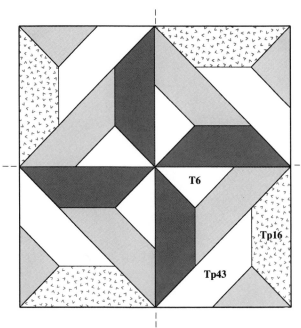

Spool Twist
12″ block
3 templates; 24 pieces
T6 (8)   Tp16 (8)   Tp43 (8)

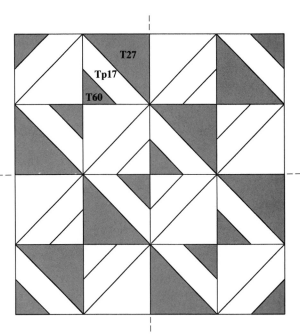

Spinning Spools
12″ block
3 templates; 48 pieces
T27 (16)   T60 (16)   Tp17 (16)

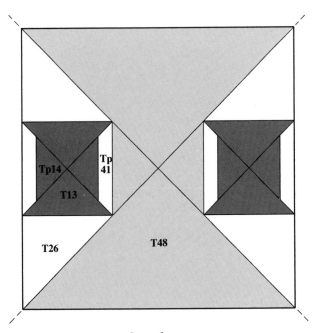

Spools
12″ block
5 templates; 20 pieces
T13 (6)   T26 (4)   Tp41 (4)
T14 (4)   T48 (2)

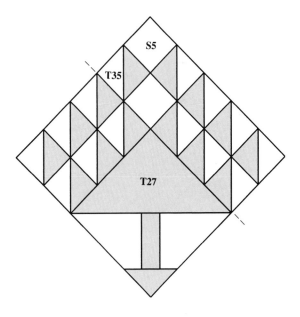

Pine Tree
6″ block
3 templates; 32 pieces
(appliqué, stem and base; ½″ bias)
T27 (1 dk.; 1 lt.)   S5 (2 lt.)
T35 (14 lt.; 14 dk.)

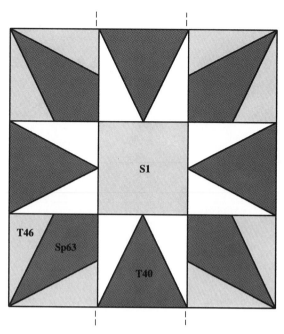

Starglow #1
12″ block
4 templates; 25 pieces
T40 (4)   S1 (1)   Sp63 (4)
T46 (8dk; 8lt)

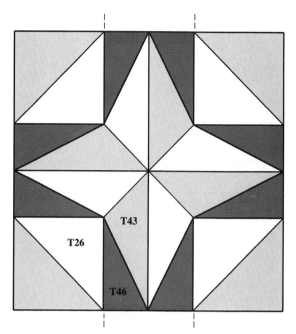

Starglow #2
12″ block
3 templates; 24 pieces
T26 (8)   T43 (8)   T46 (8)

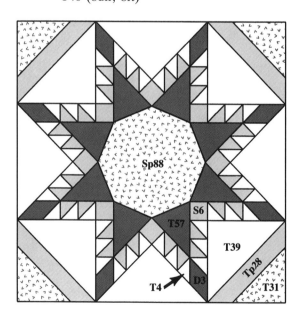

Feathered Star
20″ block
8 templates; 121 pieces
T4 (32 dk.; 48 lt.) grainline #1
T31 (4)   T57 (8)   S6 (8)   Sp88 (1)
T39 (8)   Tp28 (4)   D3 (8)

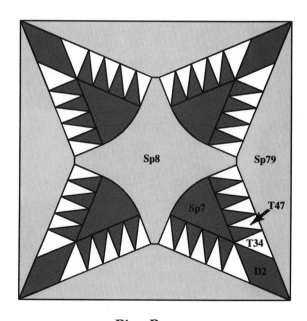

Pine Burr
18″ block
6 templates; 85 pieces
T34 (8)   D2 (4)   Sp7 (4)   Sp79 (4)
T47 (32 lt.; 32 dk.)   Sp8 (1)

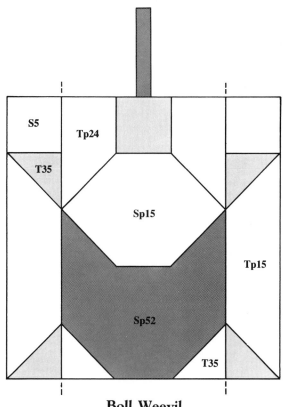

Boll Weevil
5″ block
6 templates; 15 pieces (appliqué snout; 1¼″ long)
T35 (4 dk.; 2 lt.) Tp24 (2 lt.) Sp15 (1)
Tp15 (2 lt.) S5 (2 lt.; 1 dk.) Sp52 (1)

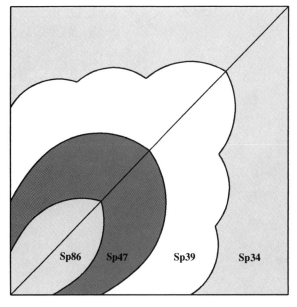

Cotton Boll Swag Corner
10″ block
4 templates; 8 pieces
Sp34 (2) Sp39 (2) Sp47 (2) Sp86 (2)

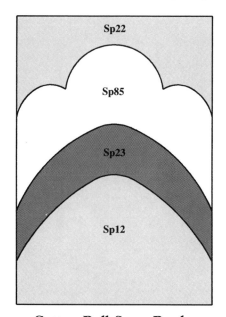

Cotton Boll Swag Border
7″ x 10″ block
4 templates; 4 pieces
Sp12 (1) Sp22 (1) Sp23 (1) Sp85 (1)

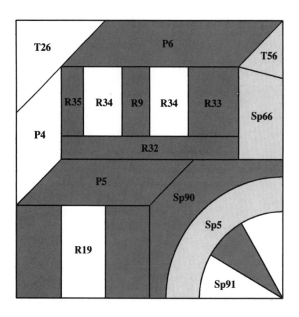

The Haunted Mill of Willow Creek
12″ block
15 templates; 20 pieces

T26 (1)	R32 (1)	P4 (1)	Sp66 (1)
T56 (1)	R33 (1)	P5 (1)	Sp90 (1)
R9 (1)	R34 (2)	P6 (1)	Sp91 (3)
R19 (3)	R35 (1)	Sp5 (1)	

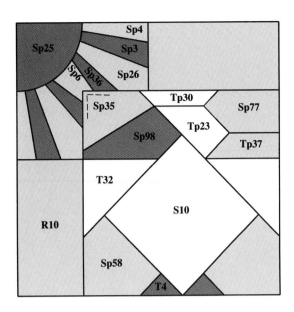

The Pelican
12″ block
17 templates; 25 pieces

T4 (2) grainline #2		Sp6 (1)	Sp58 (2)
T32 (2)	Tp37 (1)	Sp25 (1)	Sp77 (1)
R10 (2)	S10 (1)	Sp26 (2)	Sp98 (1)
Tp23 (1)	Sp3 (2)	Sp35 (1)	
Tp30 (1)	Sp4 (2)	Sp36 (2)	

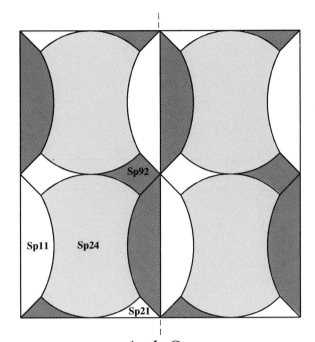

Apple Core
12″ block
4 templates; 24 pieces

Sp11 (8)   Sp21 (8)   Sp24 (4)   Sp92 (4)

Gridded Designs

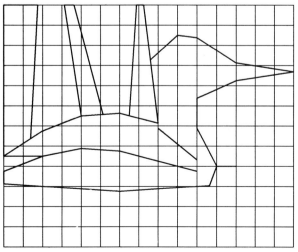

Minnesota Loon—1 square = 2″

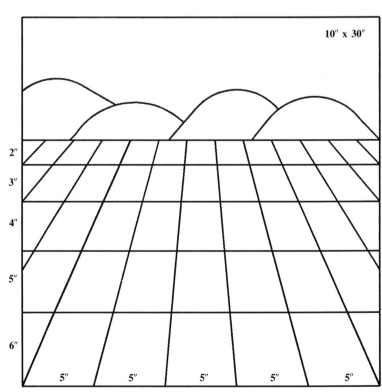

Aerial View

118

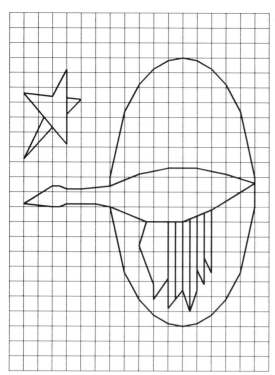

Wild Goose—1 square = 1½"

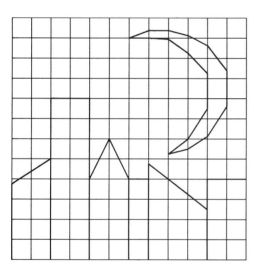

New York Skyline—1 square = 1"

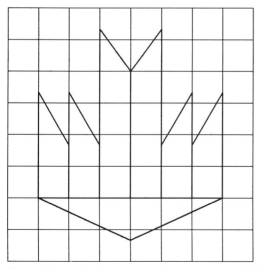

Canadian Maple Leaf—1 square = 1½"

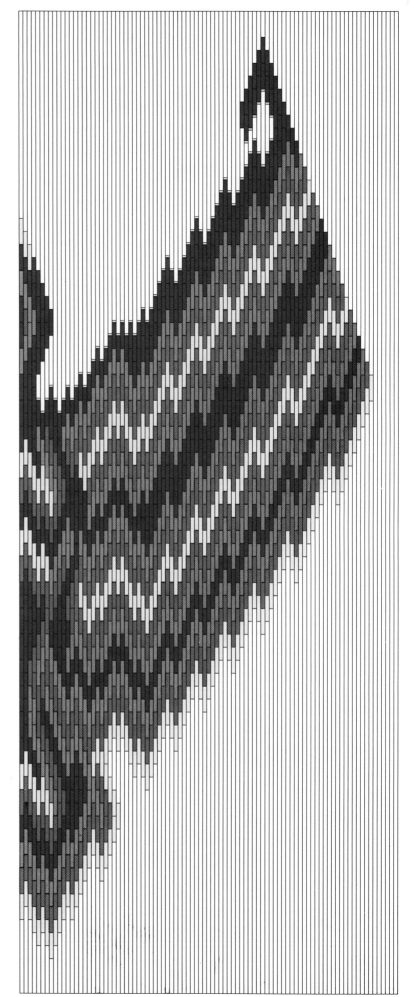

Firebird

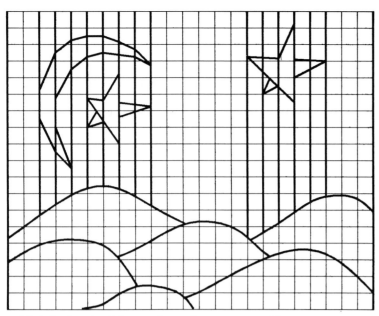

Midnight in the Mountains—1 square = 1″

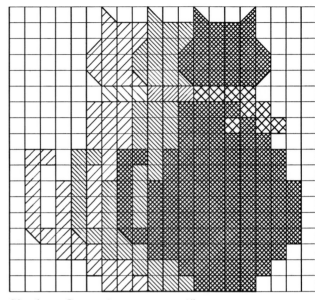

Shadow Cats—1 square = 1″

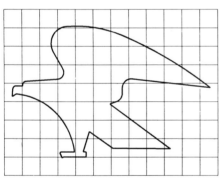

Crazy Patch Eagle—1 square = 2″

Hey Diddle Diddle—1 square = 1¼″

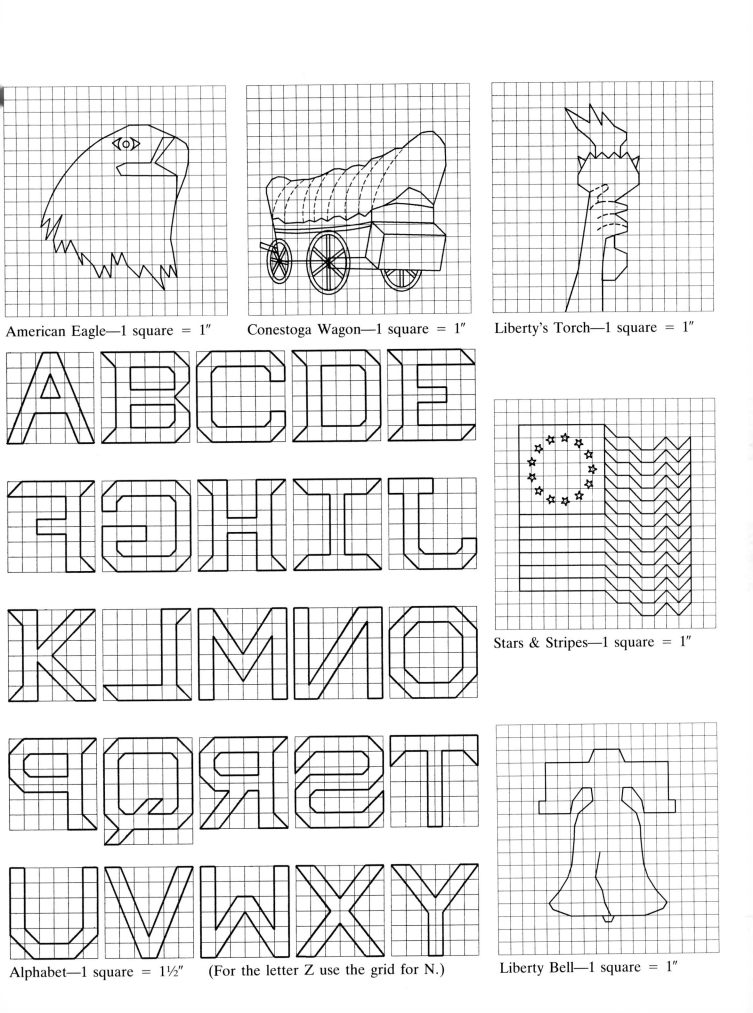

American Eagle—1 square = 1″

Conestoga Wagon—1 square = 1″

Liberty's Torch—1 square = 1″

Stars & Stripes—1 square = 1″

Alphabet—1 square = 1½″   (For the letter Z use the grid for N.)

Liberty Bell—1 square = 1″

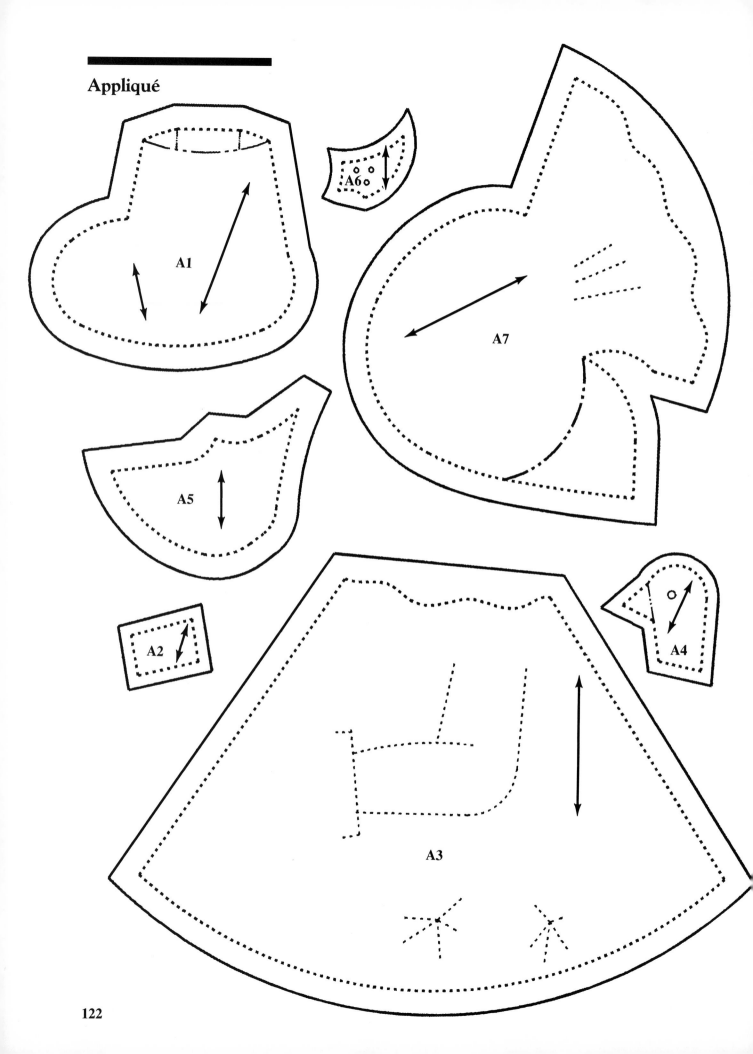

Appliqué

A1

A6

A7

A5

A2

A3

A4

Triangles

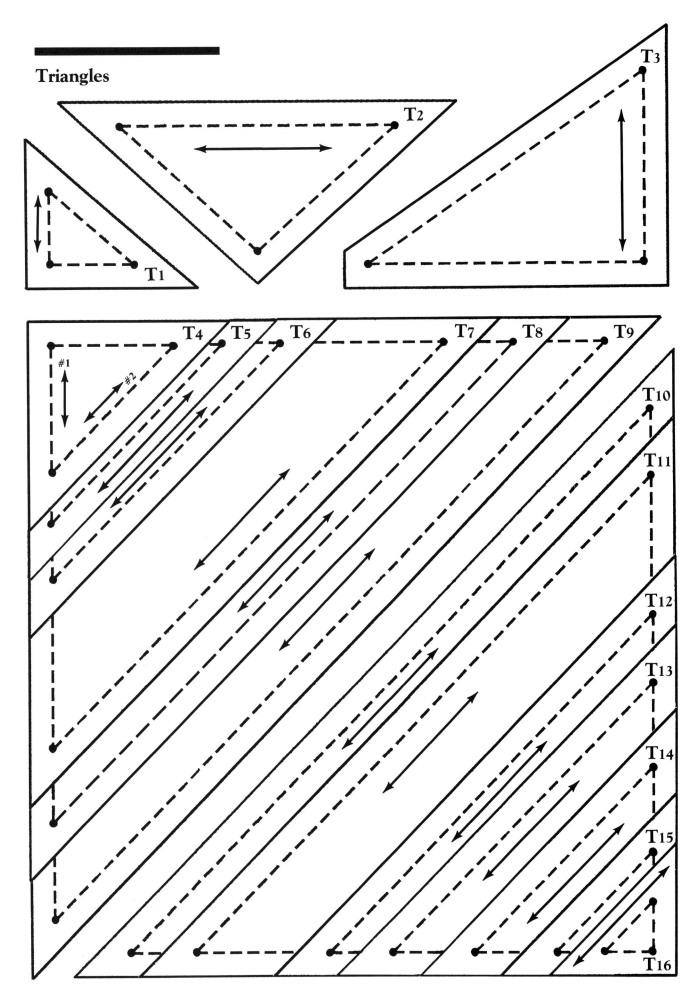

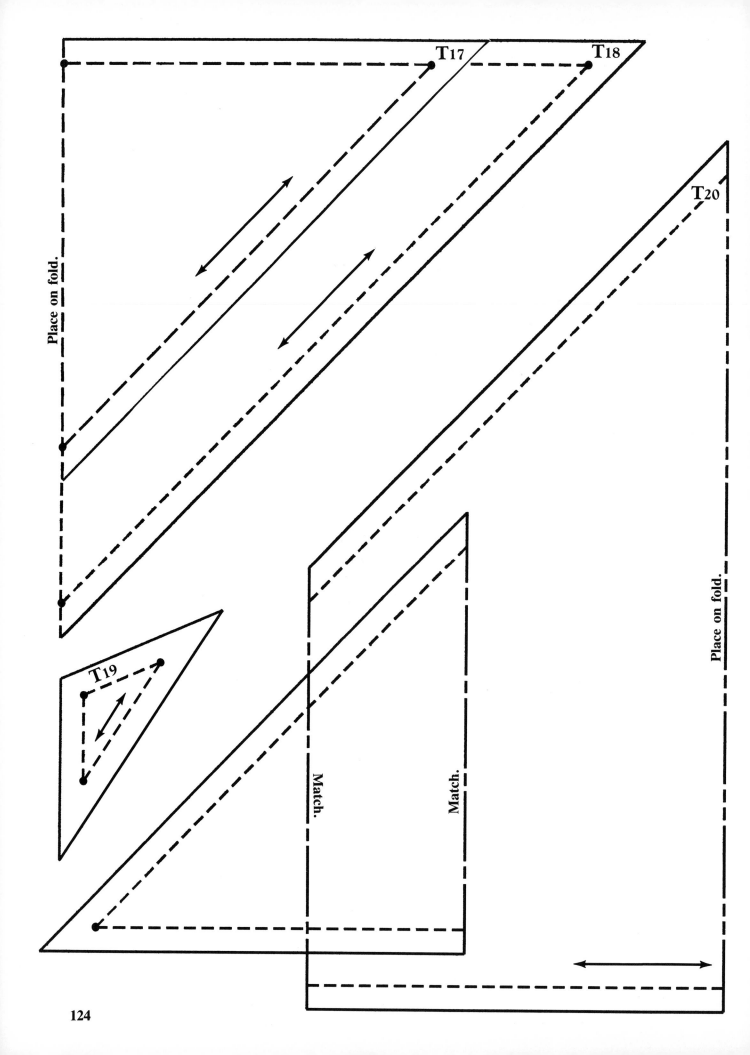

T17

T18

T20

Place on fold.

Place on fold.

T19

Match.

Match.

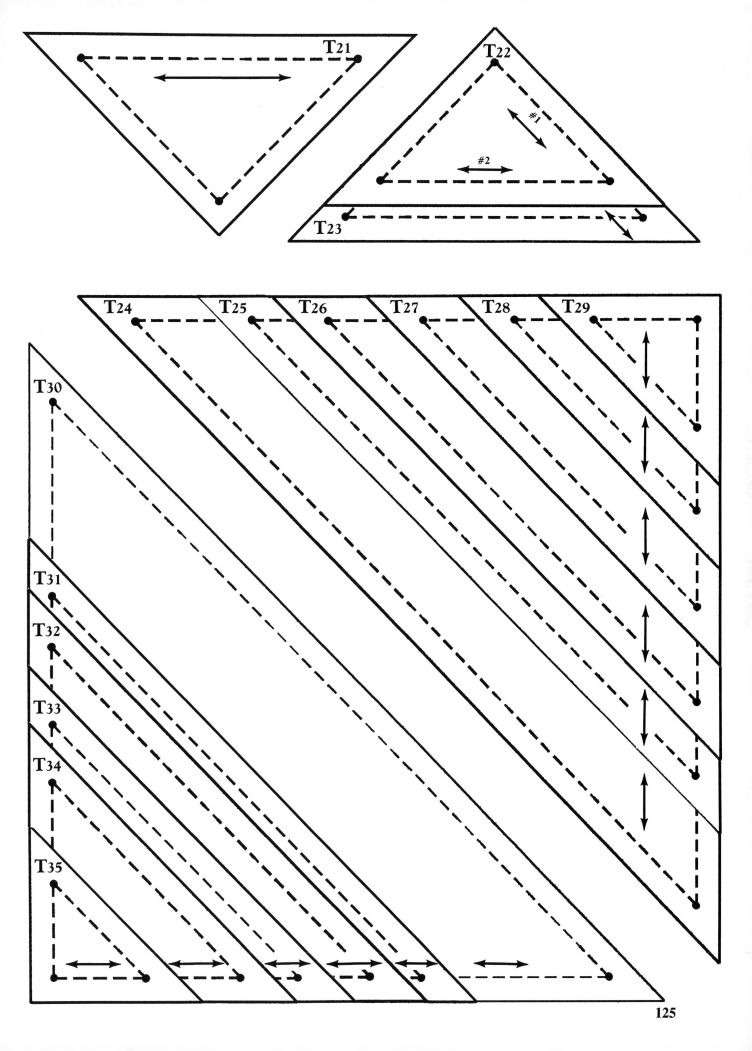

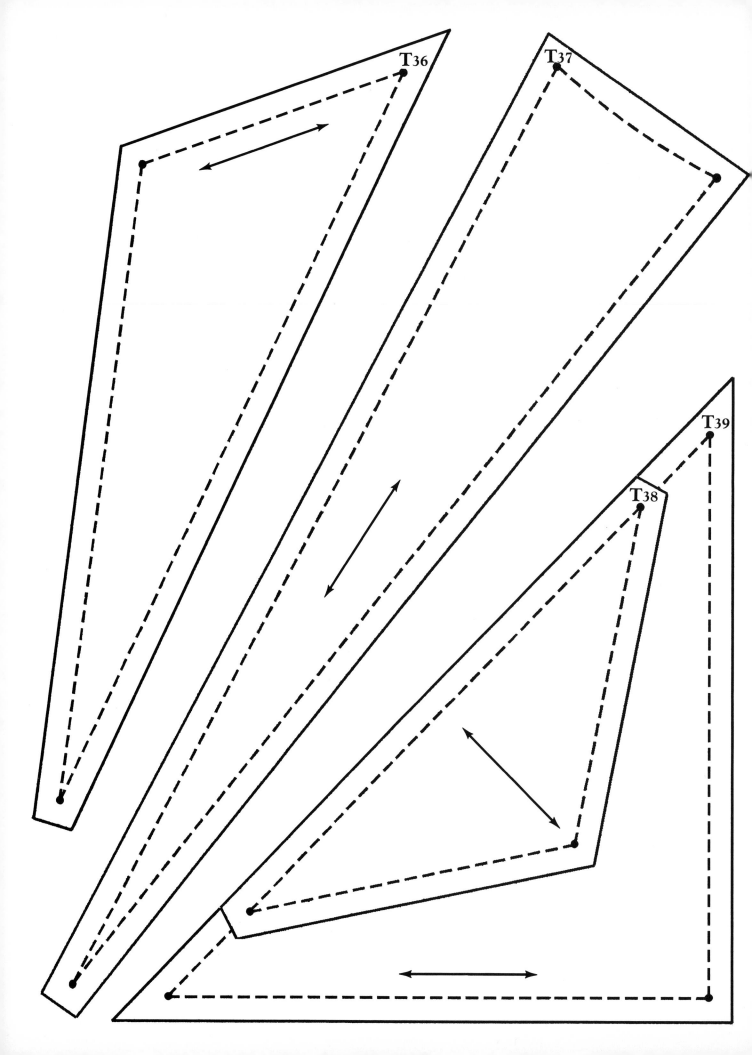

T36

T37

T39

T38

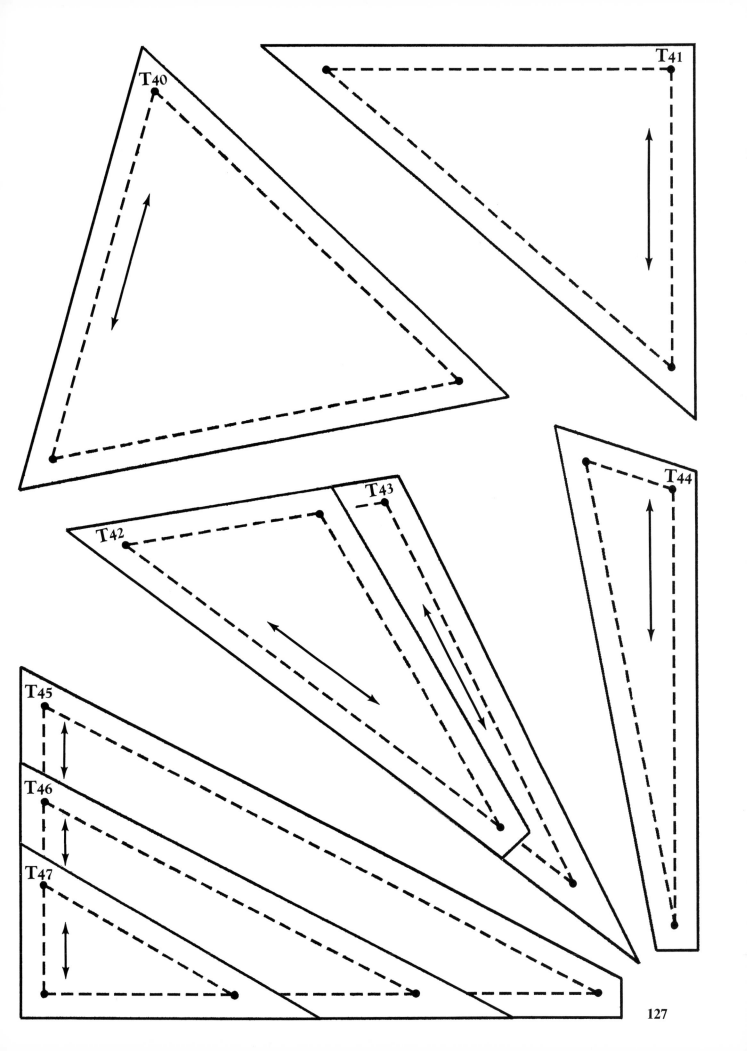

T40

T41

T42

T43

T44

T45

T46

T47

127

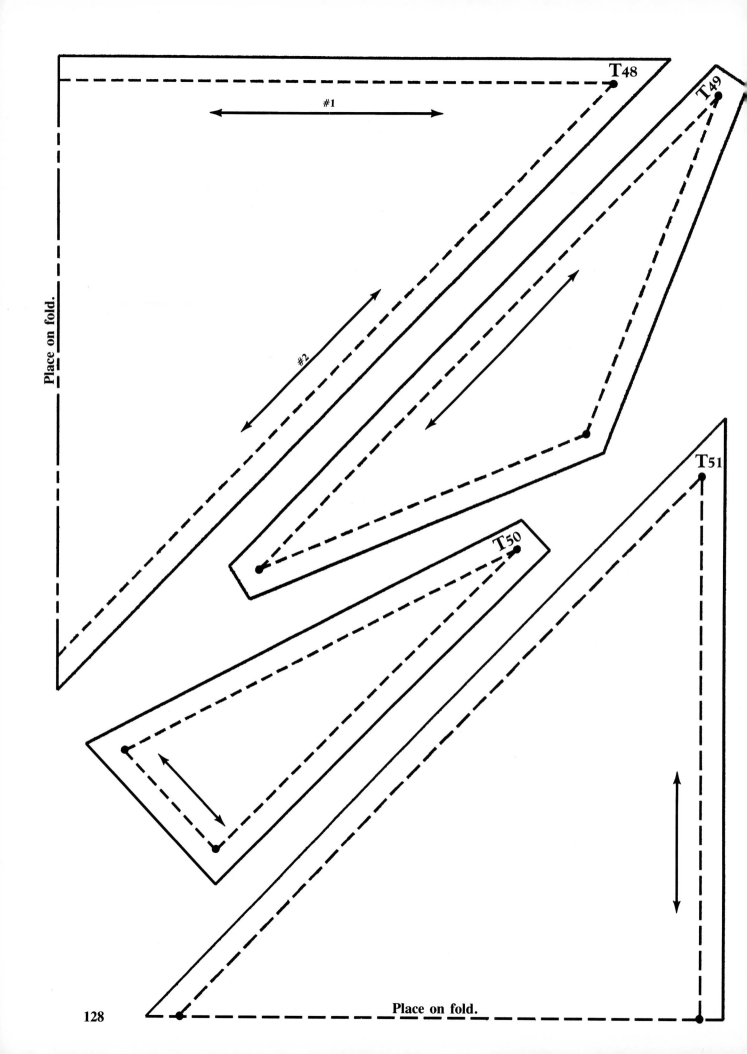

Place on fold.

T48

#1

#2

T49

T51

T50

Place on fold.

128

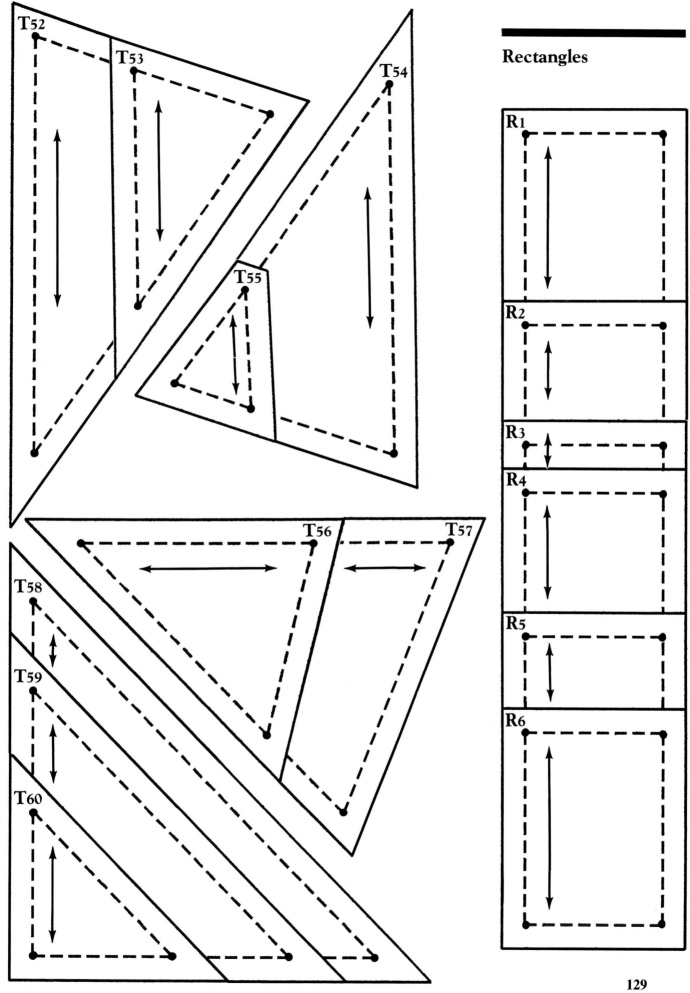

Rectangles

129

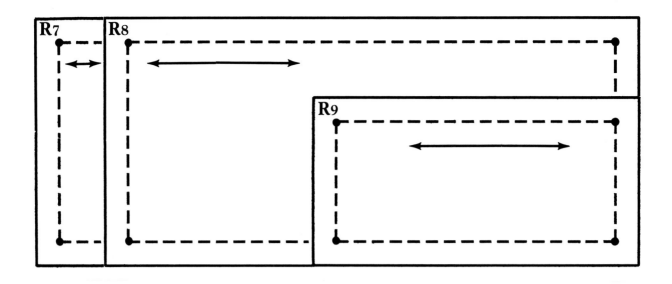

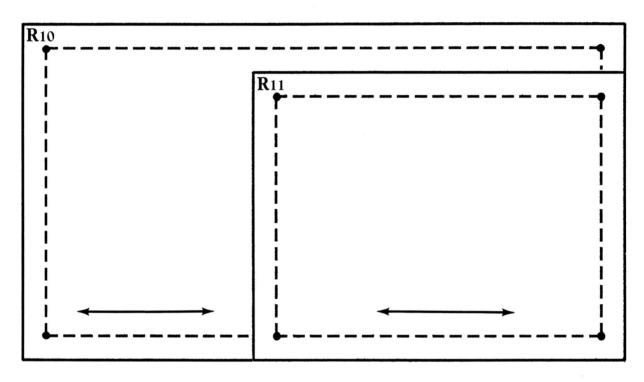

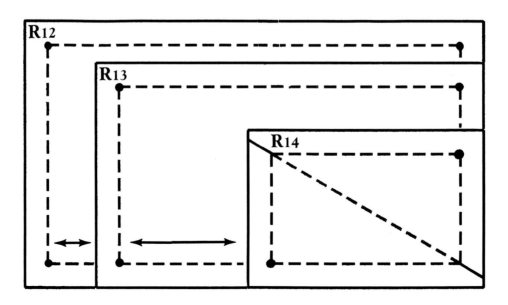

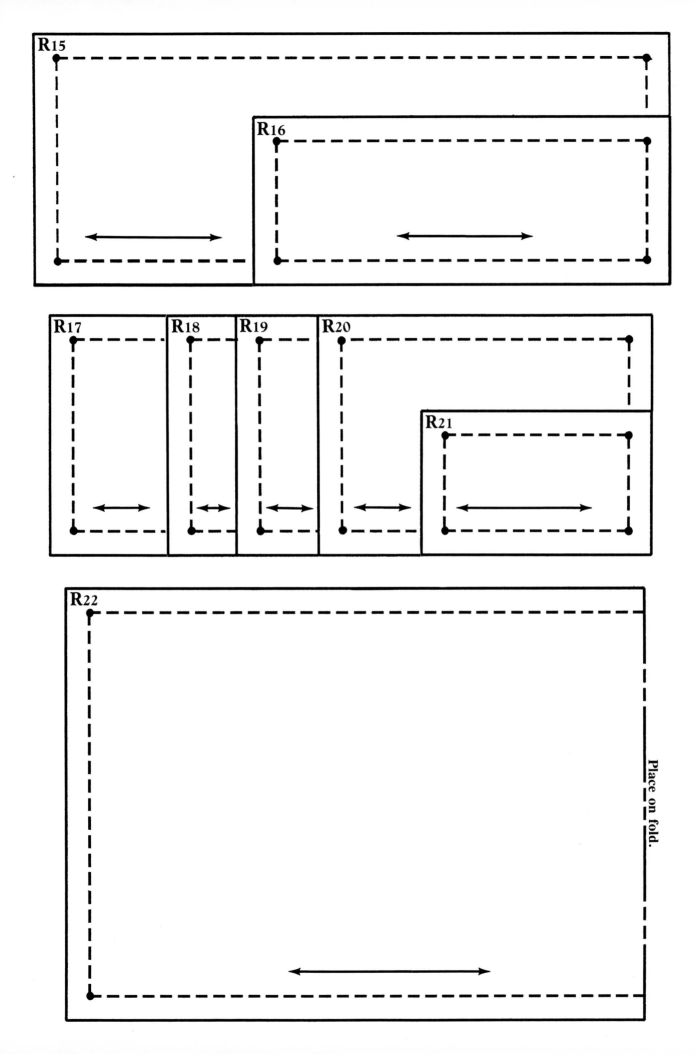

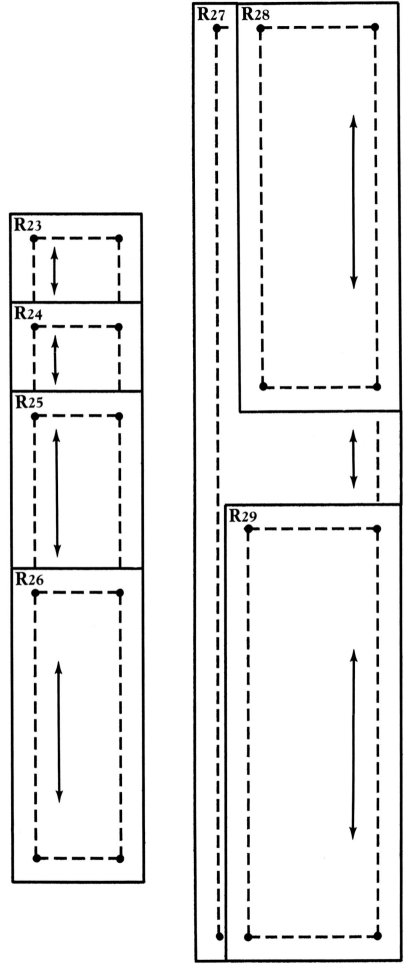

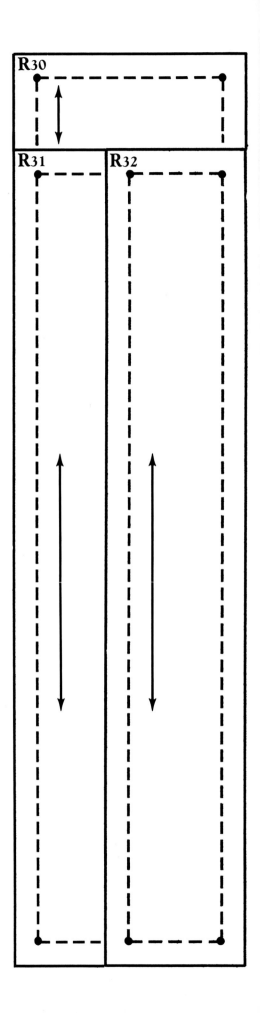

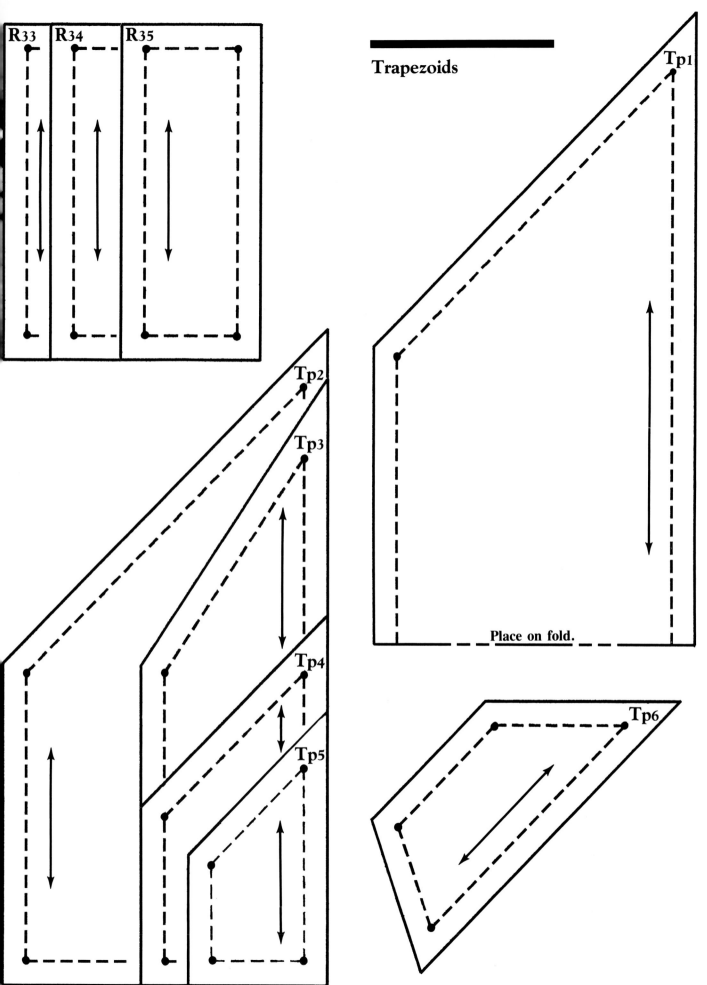

Trapezoids

R33 R34 R35

Tp1

Tp2

Tp3

Tp4

Tp5

Place on fold.

Tp6

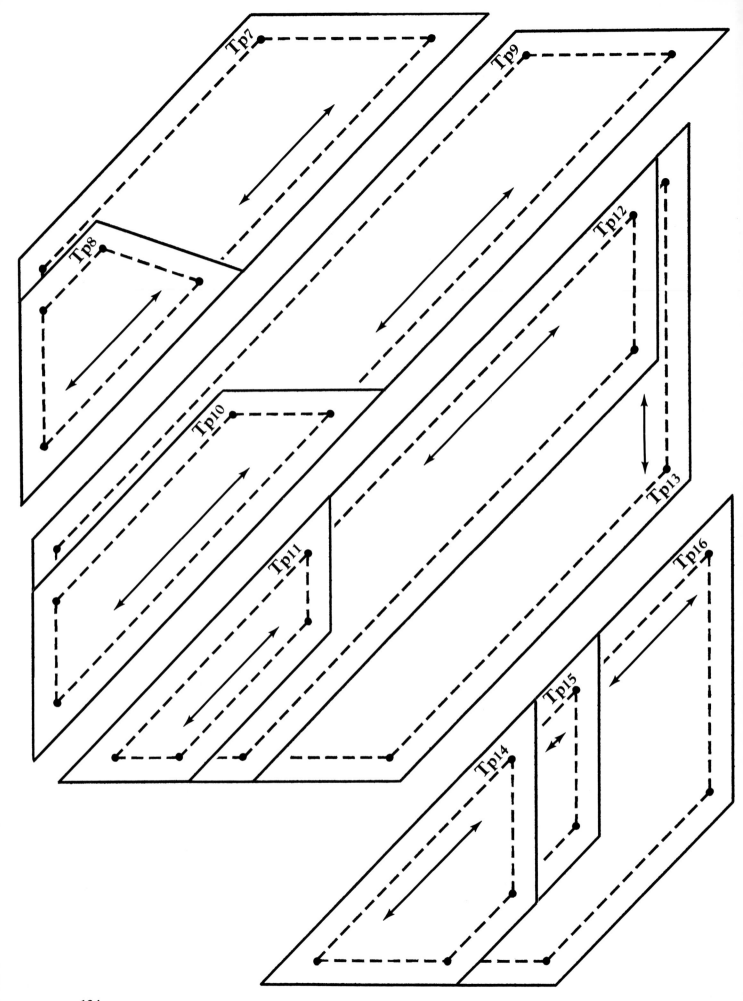

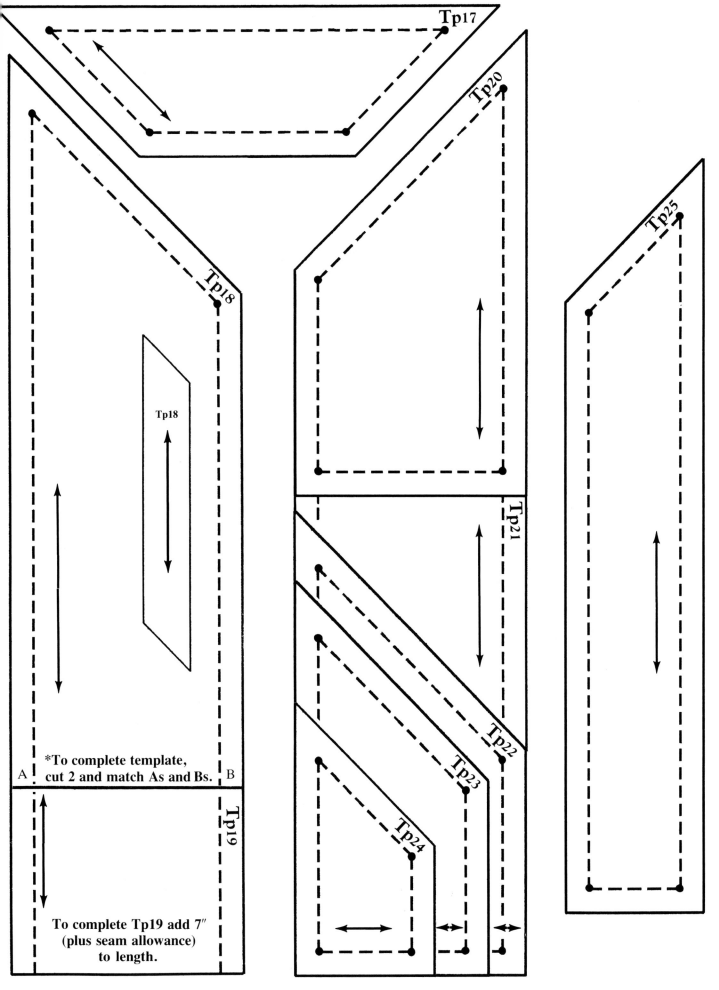

Tp17

Tp20

Tp25

Tp18

Tp18

Tp21

A | B

*To complete template,
cut 2 and match As and Bs.

Tp19

Tp22

Tp23

Tp24

To complete Tp19 add 7″
(plus seam allowance)
to length.

135

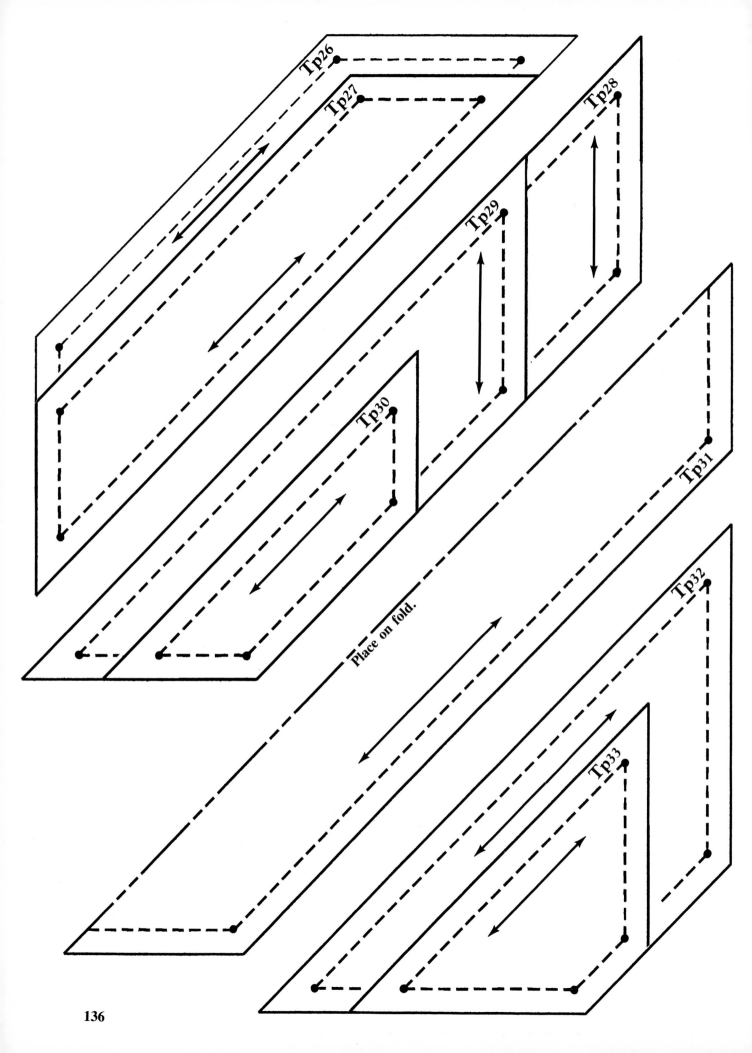

Tp26
Tp27
Tp28
Tp29
Tp30
Tp31
Tp32
Tp33

Place on fold.

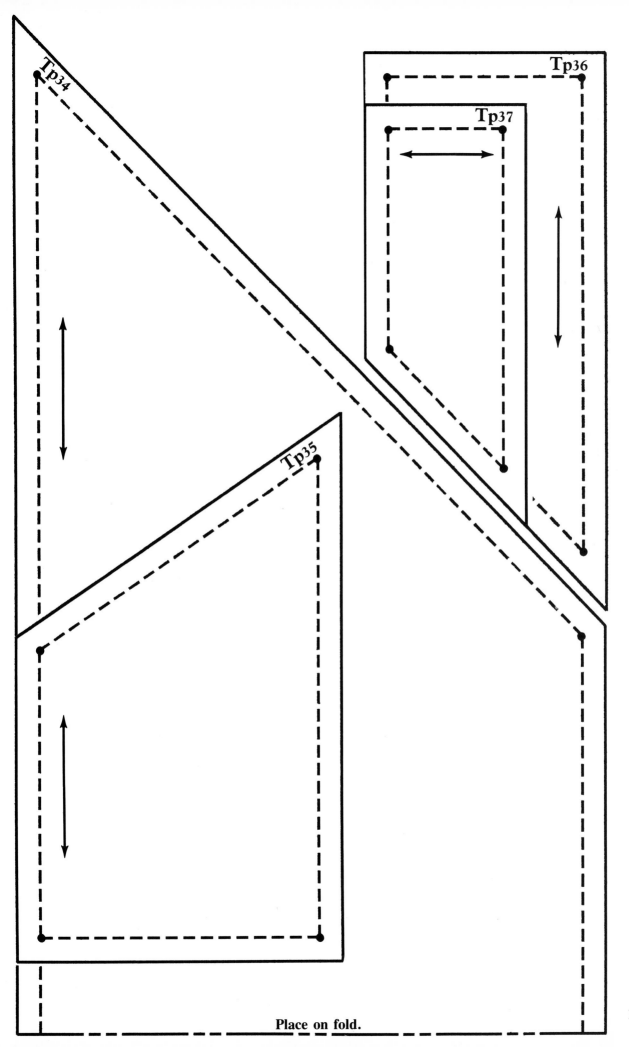

Tp34

Tp36

Tp37

Tp35

Place on fold.

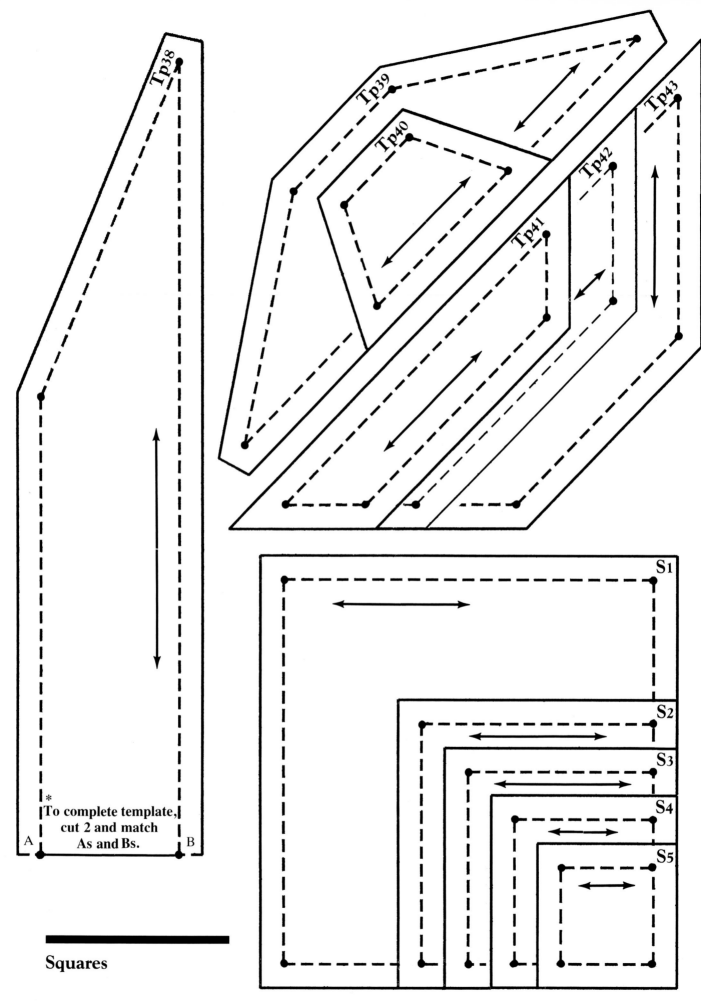

Tp38

Tp39

Tp40

Tp41

Tp42

Tp43

*To complete template,
cut 2 and match
As and Bs.

A   B

S1

S2

S3

S4

S5

Squares

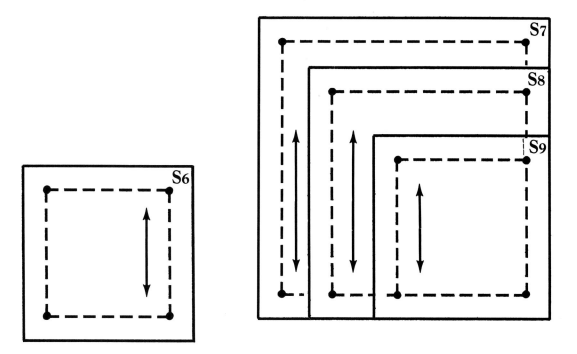

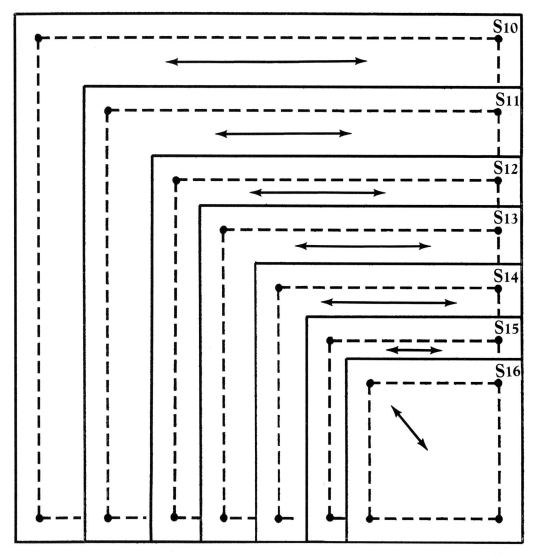

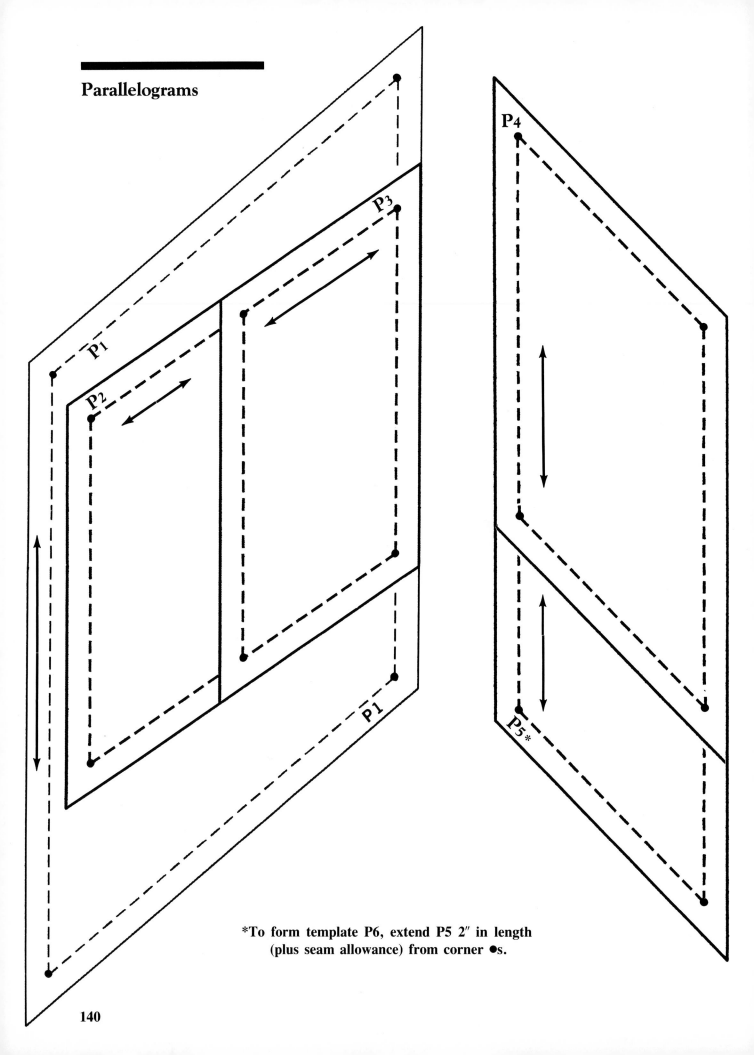

Parallelograms

P1

P2

P3

P1

P4

P5*

*To form template P6, extend P5 2″ in length
(plus seam allowance) from corner ●s.

140

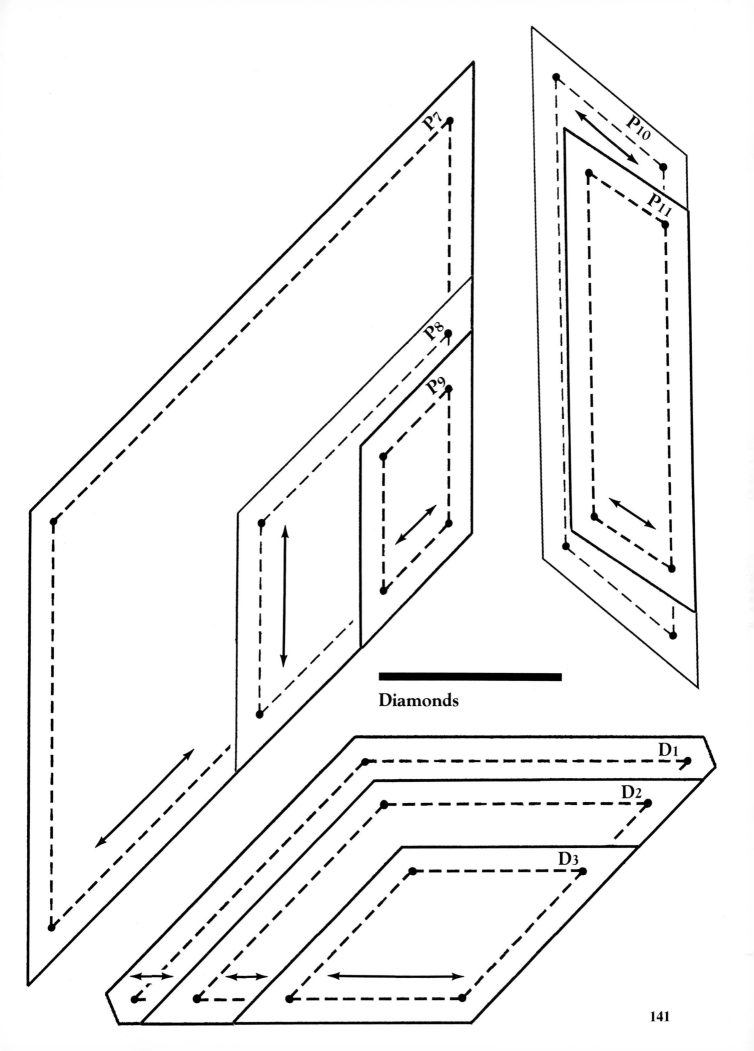

Diamonds

P7 P8 P9 P10 P11

D1 D2 D3

Special Pieces

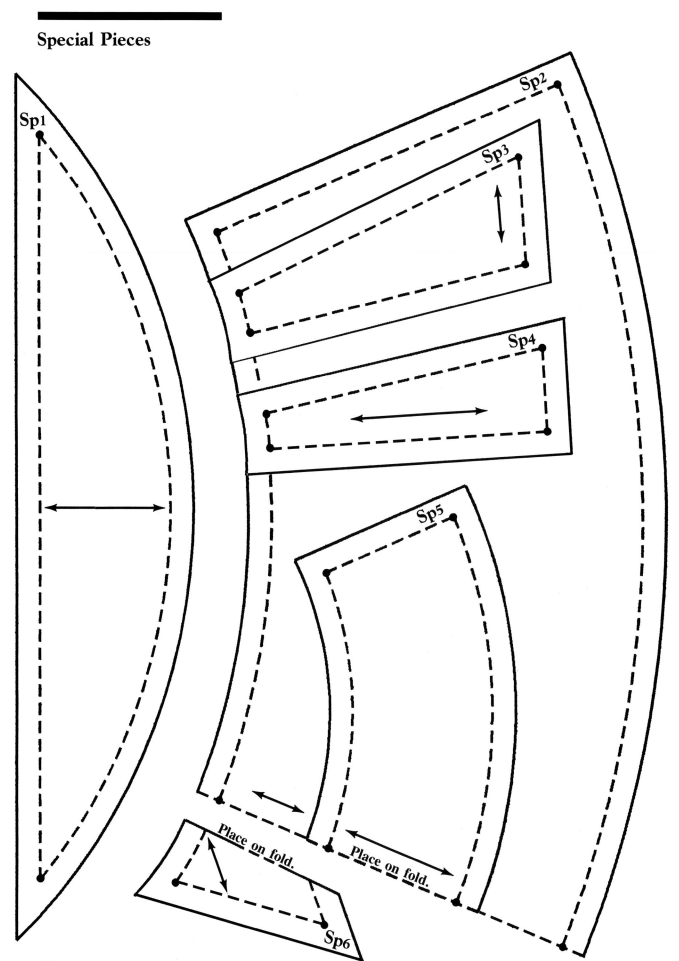

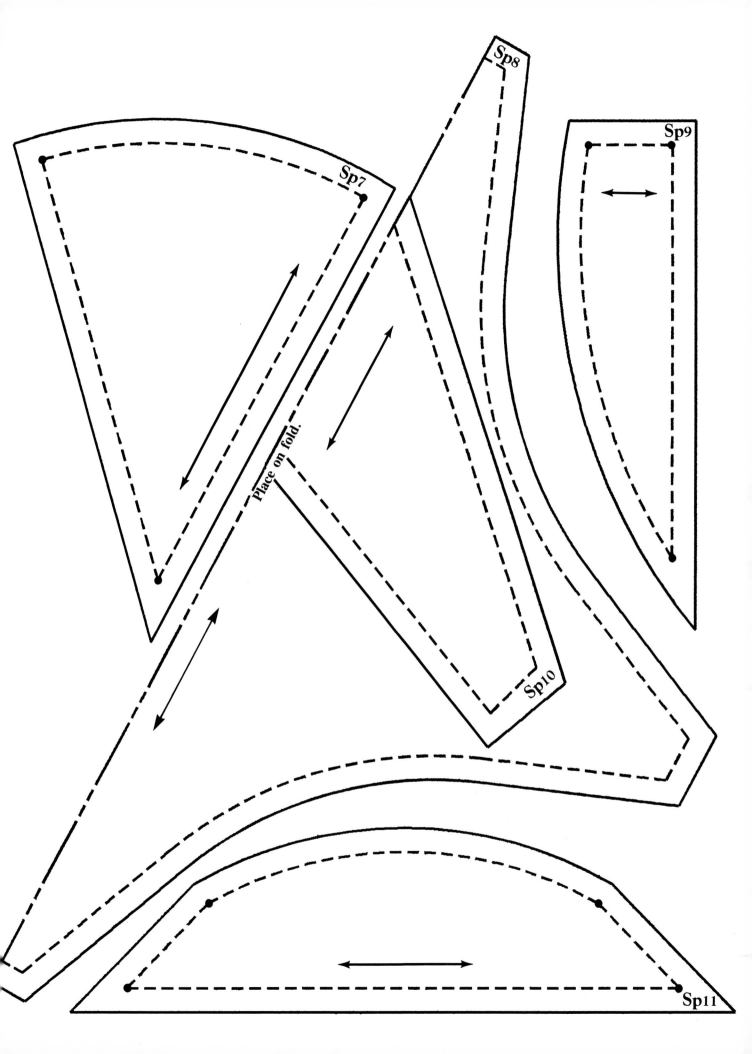

Sp8

Sp9

Sp7

Place on fold.

Sp10

Sp11

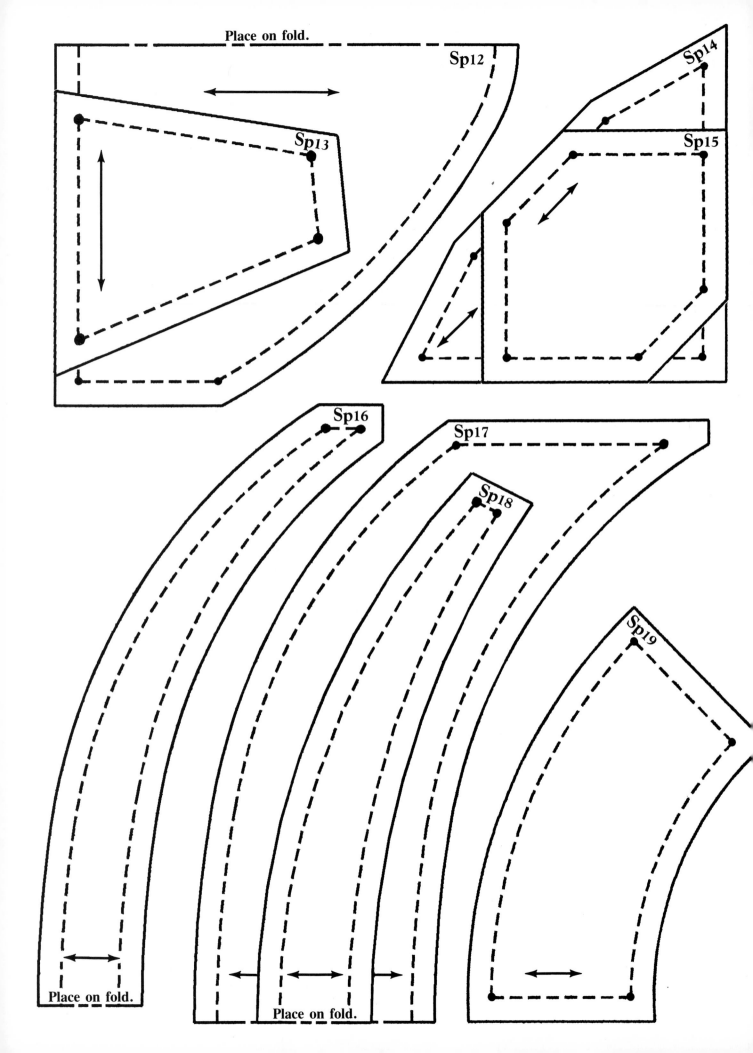

Place on fold.

Sp12

Sp13

Sp14

Sp15

Sp16

Sp17

Sp18

Sp19

Place on fold.

Place on fold.

Place on fold.

Sp20

Sp21

Sp22

Sp23

Place on fold.

Sp24

Sp25

145

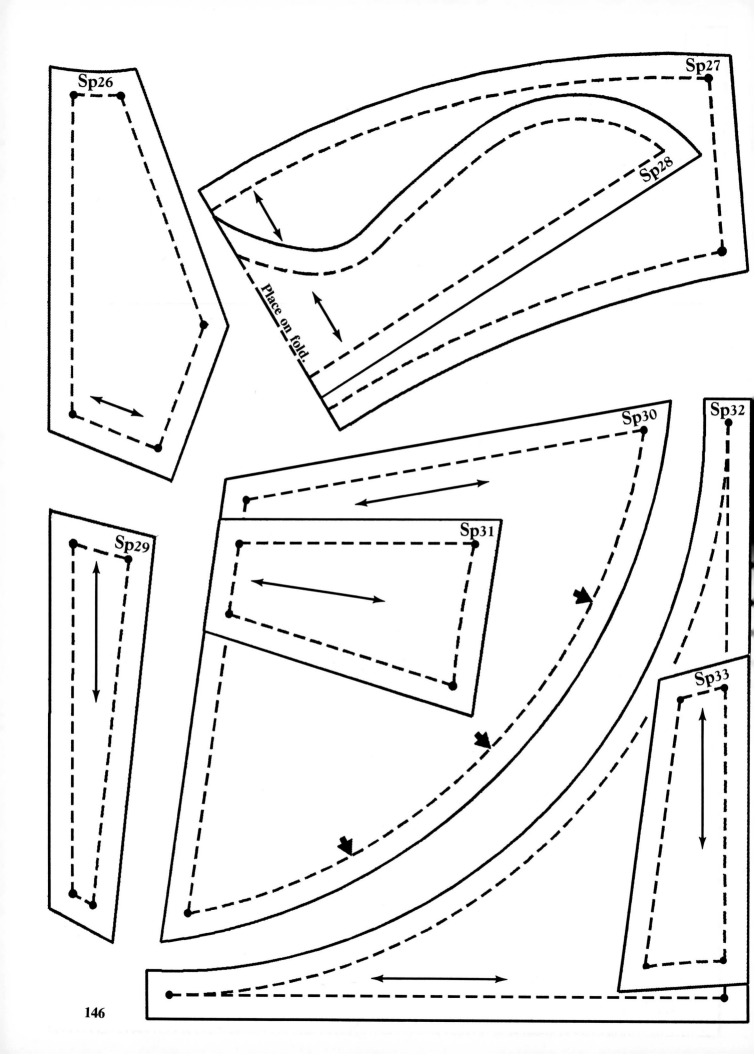

Sp26

Sp27

Sp28

Place on fold.

Sp29

Sp30

Sp31

Sp32

Sp33

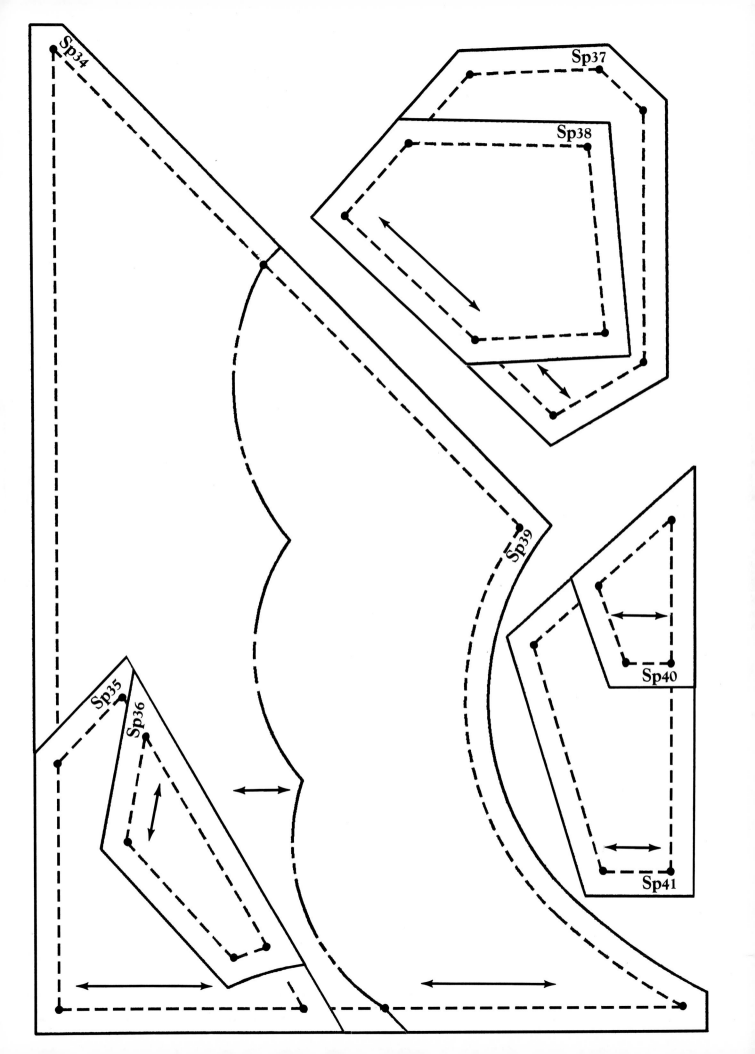

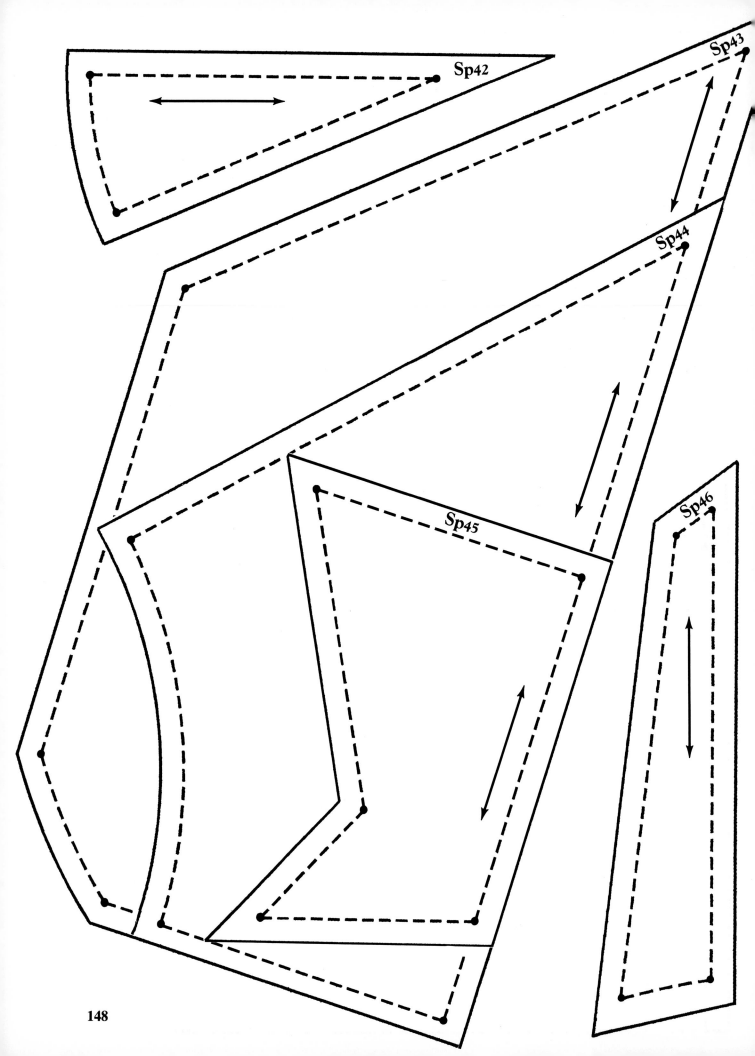

Sp42

Sp43

Sp44

Sp45

Sp46

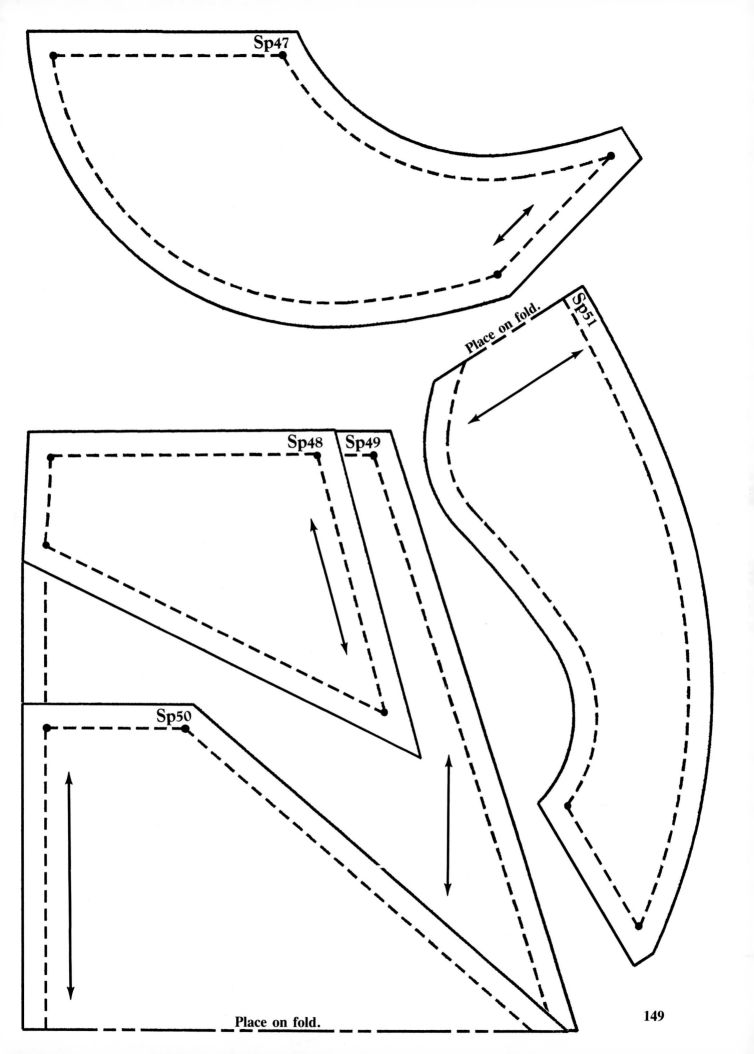

Sp47

Sp51

Place on fold.

Sp48

Sp49

Sp50

Place on fold.

149

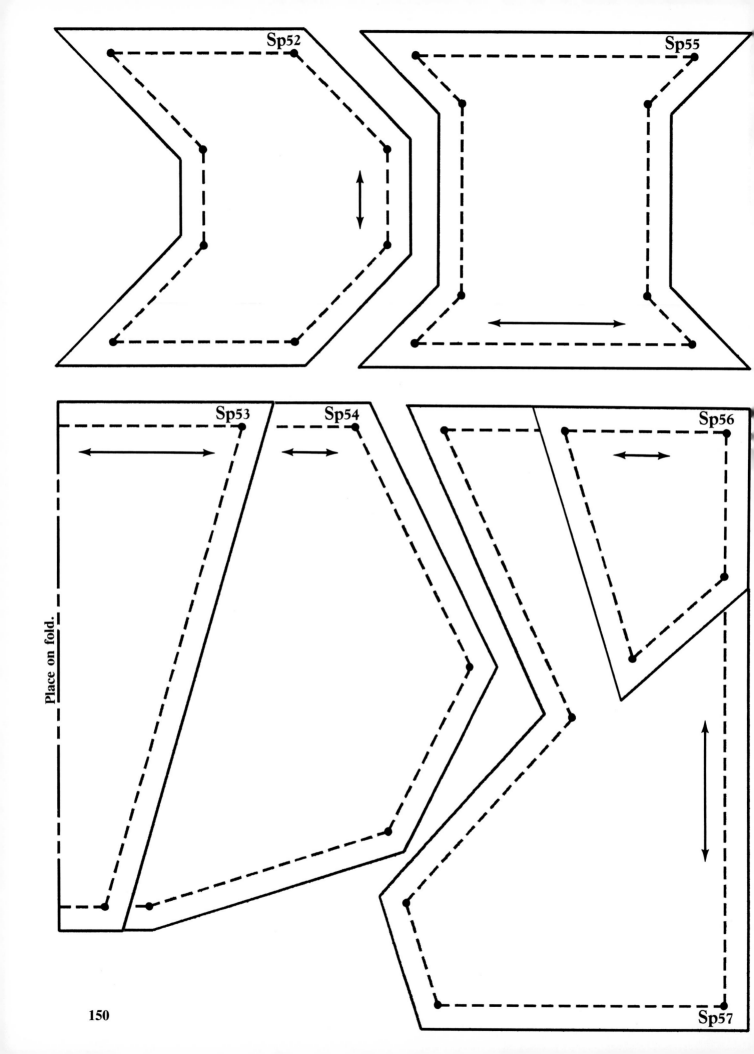

Sp52

Sp55

Sp53

Sp54

Sp56

Place on fold.

Sp57

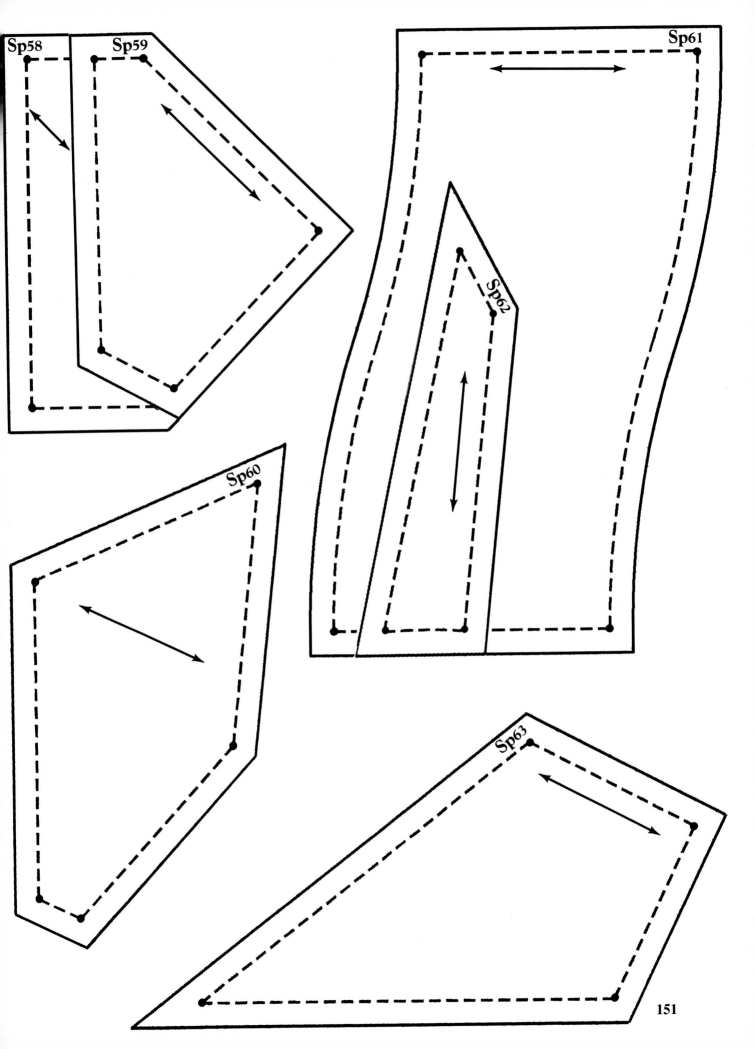

Sp58

Sp59

Sp61

Sp62

Sp60

Sp63

151

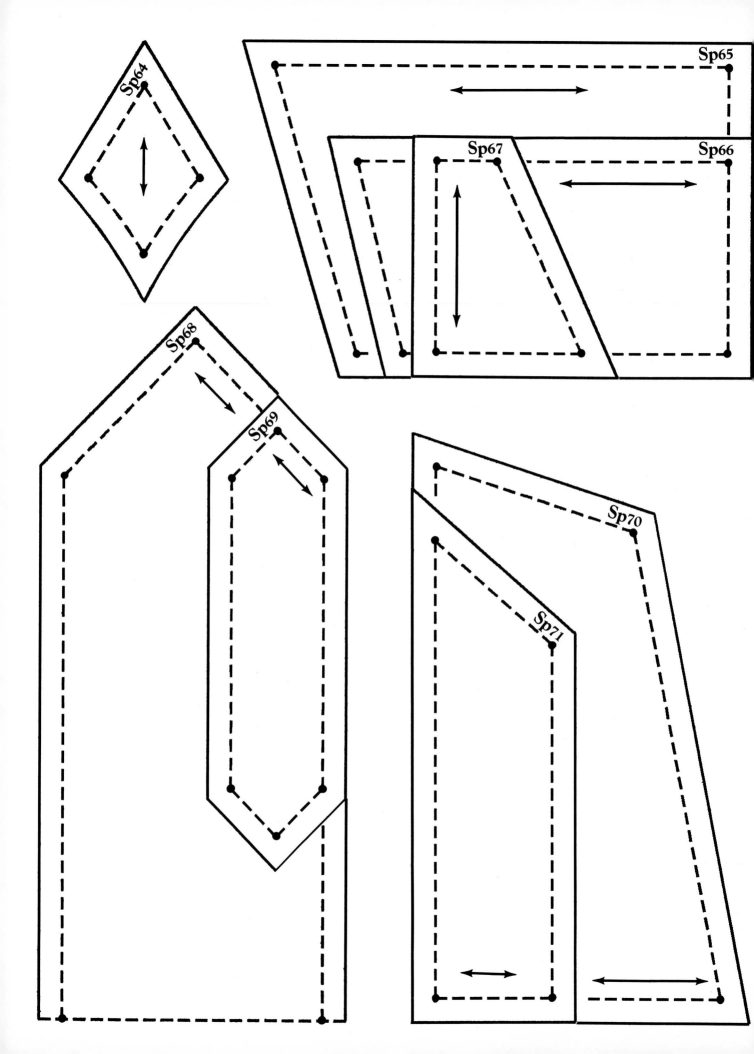

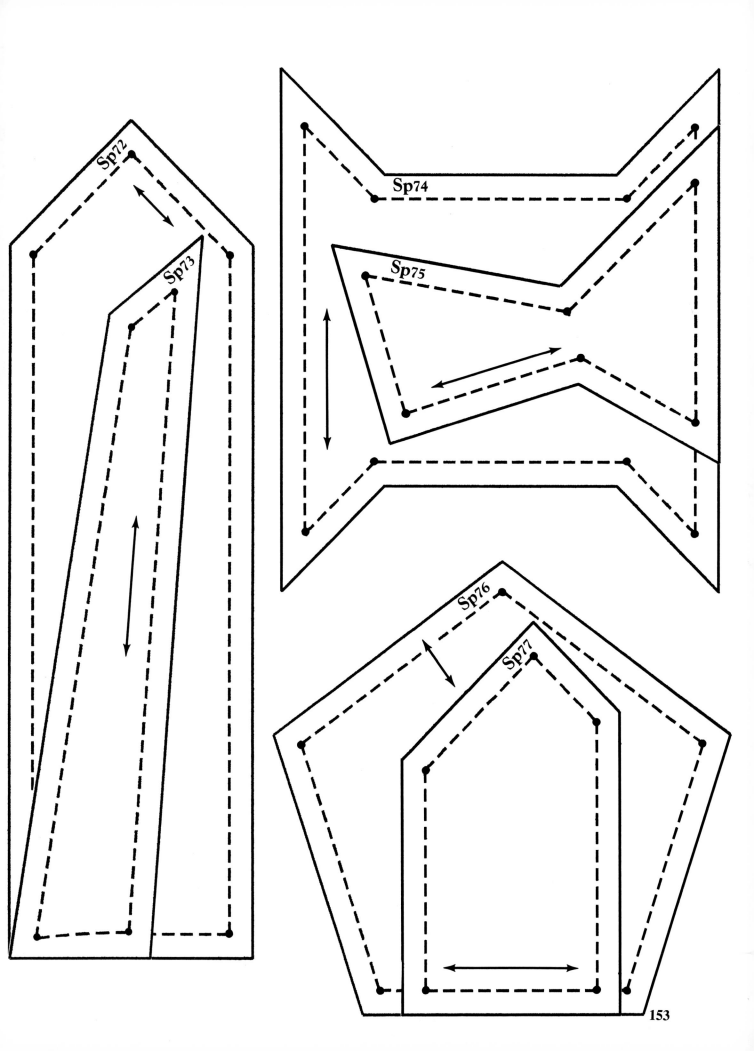

Sp72

Sp73

Sp74

Sp75

Sp76

Sp77

153

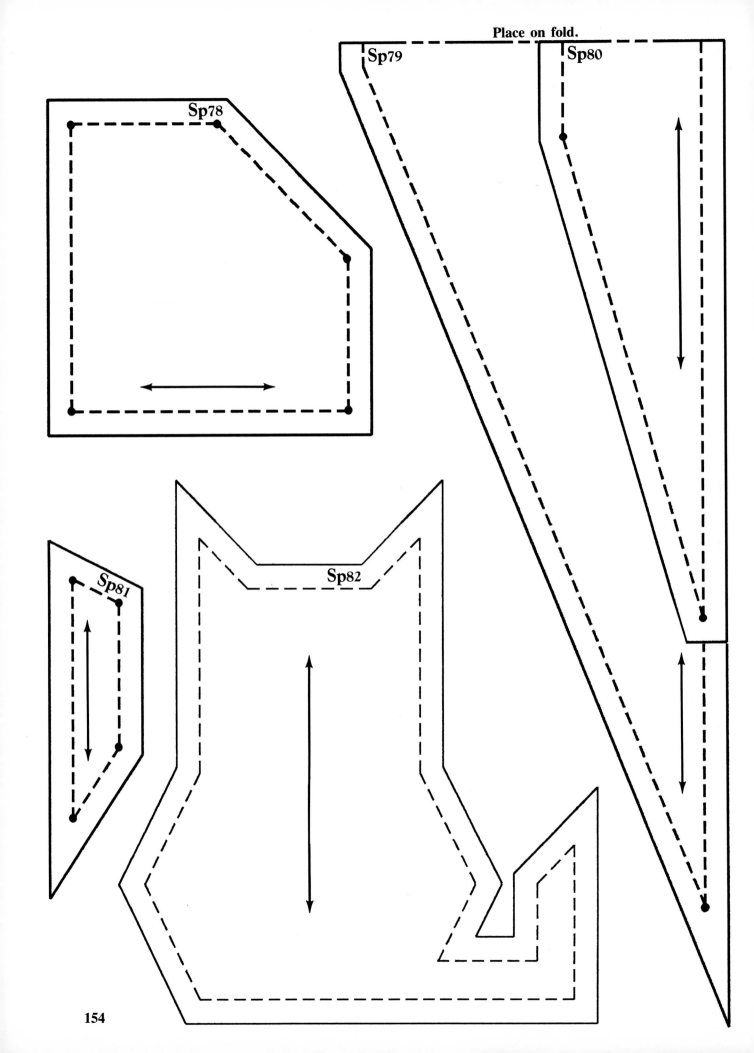

Sp78

Sp79

Place on fold.

Sp80

Sp81

Sp82

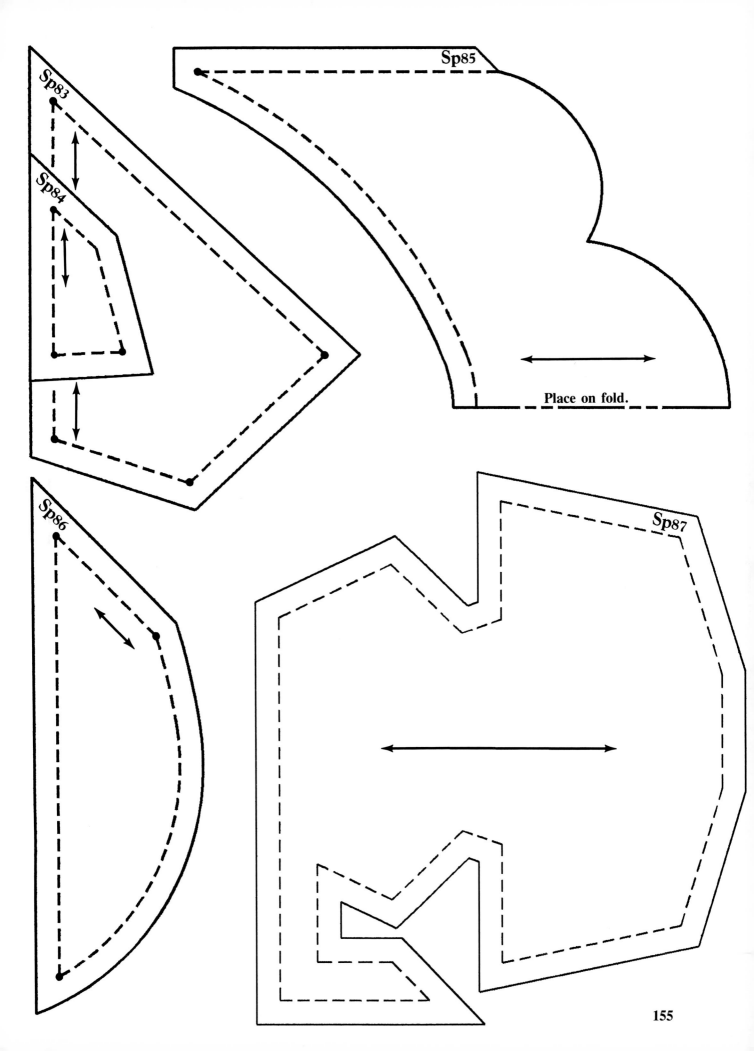

Sp83

Sp84

Sp85

Place on fold.

Sp86

Sp87

155

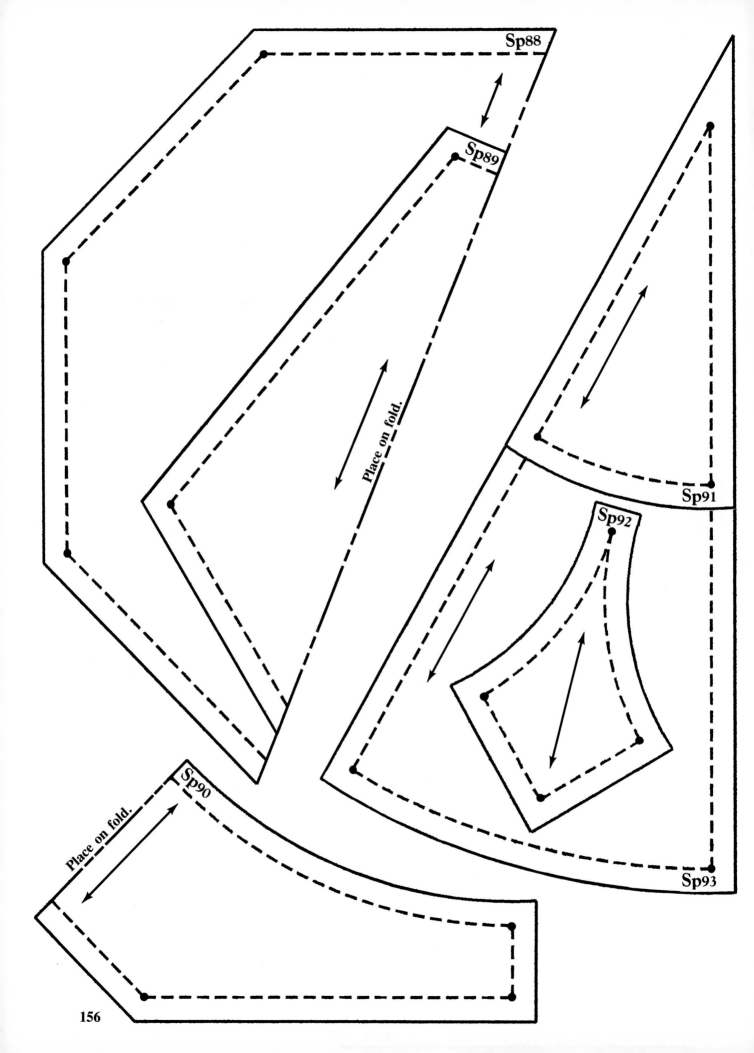

Sp88

Sp89

Place on fold.

Sp91

Sp92

Sp93

Sp90

Place on fold.

156

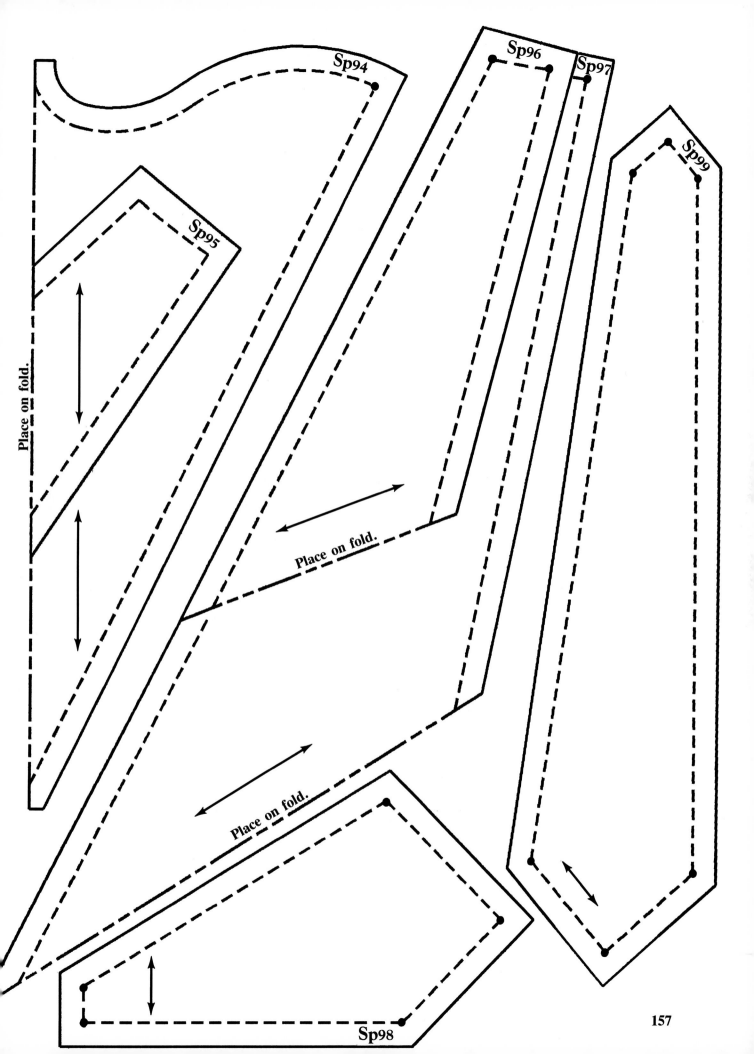

Place on fold.

Sp94

Sp96

Sp97

Sp99

Sp95

Place on fold.

Place on fold.

Sp98

157

APPENDIX

Lap quilting is a method by which a quilt is quilted one section at a time. Some designs in *New Ideas for Lap Quilting* were quilted block by block while others were quilted row by row. Broken lines extending from the quilt diagrams indicate the sections. The key to successful lap quilting is uniformity of block size. Make sure your units are the same size so that they will fit together after quilting.

Quilting Stencil Design: The stencil design is the line you follow when you are quilting. These lines are applied to the block after it is pieced or appliquéd but before it is basted to the batting and backing.

There are two types of stencil or quilting lines—contrary and compatible. Contrary lines create a new secondary design. They don't follow the lines of the piecework or appliqué. This new pattern of quilted stitches should enhance and not detract.

Compatible, or outline, quilting is the traditonal form of quilting. These quilting stitches echo the lines created by seams or turned-under edges.

Several tools, such as pencils, chalk markers, soap slivers, water-erasable pens, or soapstone markers, can be used to transfer the stencil lines to the fabric. (Always test markers for easy removal.) Also popular today are precut stencils or stencils that you make yourself from plastic. Masking tape is a handy implement to use as a stitching guide. Apply it after the block is basted.

When planning your quilting design, keep in mind that the quilting pattern should flow from the center outward and the amount of quilting in the separate sections must be consistent.

Basting: Cut batting and backing the same size as your quilt block. Baste all three layers—block, batting, and backing—together before quilting.

Backing fabric is of primary importance in lap quilting. A print helps to hide the handmade connections on the back.

Align the corners of all three layers and pin in place. Using a contrasting thread, take long basting stitches. Baste in a pinwheel fashion and around the outside edges.

Quilting: For lap quilting, leave at least ½″ free of quilting on all outside edges. With all forms of quilting, use hidden knots, and the fewer the better.

Hand quilting with or without a frame or hoop requires a running stitch. The needle enters the layers at an angle, while the fingers of the "off" hand ensure that all three layers are caught in each stitch. In this method of quilting, the bottom stitches can become slightly displaced. I would encourage you to use a thimble and something to protect the "off" finger that is acting as a guide underneath the block. Do not pull the thread too tight.

When you are working with a supported hoop, I suggest using the rocking method of quilting. With the needle point coming towards you, steer the eye of the needle with the tip of the thimble. (An indented thimble is ideal for the job.) The thumb is out in front to balance the up-and-down rocking motion, while underneath, the other hand works to help free the material. This method produces bottom stitches that line up with the top stitches in a consistent manner. Using a supported hoop allows you to turn your work around, offering easy accessibility to all sides without the hoop rim resting inside your elbows.

A: Machine-stitch together.

Quilt Assembly: Remove basting threads, masking tape, and any fabric markings. Trim the edges so that all three layers are even. Decide on either horizontal or vertical row assembly.

In block-to-block assembly, the front or the backing of two adjoining blocks is machine-stitched, and the reverse side is hand-stitched in a flat lapped seam. Select two adjacent blocks and free the sides to be machine-stitched by pinning the batting and other layers out of the way. Align these freed edges and pin in place. Machine-stitch ¼″ from edge (Photo A).

An alternative is to include batting of bottom block in machine-stitched seam (Photo B).

Continue to sew blocks together until a row is completed, alternating direction of seams.

Position the row on a flat surface and unpin the batting and fabric. Trim batting so that it butts up to next piece of batting. (If batting is very thin, pieces can overlap.)

Smooth the loose fabric from one block over the batting. Turn under the adjacent backing ¼″ and slipstitch a flat lapped seam in place (Photo C). (Make certain the thread doesn't go through to the other side.)

In row-to-row assembly, after the rows are sewn together, they are joined. Row-to-row assembly is identical to block assembly, except that you are working with a larger amount of fabric. Pin back batting and backing to reveal sides of rows to be attached. Pin the rows together from seam to seam, staggering seams at intersections. Some easing may be

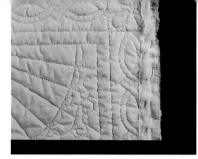

B: Include batting in seam.

C: Slipstitch blocks together.

necessary. Basting will help when sewing this long row. (If batting from one side is included, you might try using a walking foot on the sewing machine.) Backstitch at the beginning and end of each row.

After the rows are joined, the flat lapped seam is sewn as in block-to-block assembly, spreading out the rows on a flat surface.

If you are using a thin batting, another option for a lap-quilted connection might be to machine-stitch all the layers together (batting against feed dogs of the machine) except one. Then turn the unattached side under ¼″, covering the machine stitching line. Slipstitch in place.

Once the quilt is assembled, extra quilting may be needed at connection points. This will require the use of a hoop.

Binding: Bias binding is most often used to finish the edge of a quilt. The perimeter measurement listed for each quilt indicates how much bias is needed for the binding. It is best to use a double-folded bias binding for strength and durability.

Hand-baste the outside edges of the quilt together. Cut the bias 2½″ wide and fold it in half with raw edges aligned. Press lightly. Machine-stitch the entire folded bias strip to the quilt top with a ¼″ seam allowance.

After bias strip is sewn to the top, roll it over the raw edges and slipstitch in place just beyond the machine stitching on the back of the quilt.

DESIGNERS & CONTRIBUTORS